MBA Companion

for use with

Financial Accounting

Fourth Edition

Robert Libby
Cornell University – Ithaca

Patricia A. Libby
Ithaca College

Daniel G. Short
Miami University – Oxford

Prepared by
Peggy Bishop Lane
Catherine Schrand
Both of University of Pennsylvania

 Irwin

Boston   Burr Ridge, IL   Dubuque, IA   Madison, WI   New York   San Francisco   St. Louis
Bangkok   Bogotá   Caracas   Kuala Lumpur   Lisbon   London   Madrid   Mexico City
Milan   Montreal   New Delhi   Santiago   Seoul   Singapore   Sydney   Taipei   Toronto

MBA Companion for use with
FINANCIAL ACCOUNTING
Libby, Libby, Short

1 2 3 4 5 6 7 8 9 0 QPD/QPD 0 9 8 7 6 5 4 3

ISBN 0-07-255388-X

www.mhhe.com

The McGraw-Hill Companies

TABLE OF CONTENTS

MBA Supplement

FOCUS COMPANY:
FRONTIER AIRLINES

BUSINESS BACKGROUND
Frontier Airlines, founded in 1994, operates out of their hub at Denver International Airport. Frontier's business strategy is to provide affordable airfares in high volume markets. In its 2001 10-K, Frontier indicates that its near term business strategy is to increase demand for its existing routes and to expand the Denver hub operations, continuing as a regional carrier.

Frontier leases its planes using non-cancelable lease agreements. There are many reasons why a firm might choose to lease rather than buy assets. Two important considerations, especially for assets such as aircraft, are the minimal initial cash outlay and the flexibility inherent in a lease as technology changes. As described in its 2001 Annual Report, Frontier plans to begin replacing leased aircraft with purchased aircraft in fiscal year 2002. This change in investment strategy could be associated with a change in Frontier's current financial condition or it could signal a change in Frontier's expectations for the future. Lease expense is one of Frontier's most significant expenses at 17.1% of revenue. Despite the importance of aircraft as an "asset" and the significant commitment Frontier has made for future lease payments on these aircraft, neither the aircraft nor the associated "debt" appear on Frontier's balance sheet. Because the lease obligation is not recorded, these types of leases are often referred to as a form of "off-balance sheet financing." Lease accounting is the subject of Section I.

Frontier reported income tax expense of $33 million in 2001, roughly 38% of pretax income. But, Frontier's current taxes (its income tax "bill") for 2001 were approximately $32 million. The difference between the amount expensed and current taxes is due to Frontier's use of two different sets of tax rules, one to compute its tax bill (the rules of the Internal Revenue Code) and one to compute its tax expense on its income statement (Generally Accepted Accounting Principles). Neither of these amounts represents the cash that Frontier actually paid for income taxes in 2001; it paid approximately $22 million. Obviously, income taxes have a significant impact on both Frontier's earnings and cash flows. But, how do current taxes, tax expense, and taxes paid differ? And, where can you find each of these amounts in the financial statements? The accounting for income taxes is the subject of Section II.

1

REAL WORLD EXCERPT
FRONTIER AIRLINES, INC. Balance Sheets, March 31, 2001 and 2000

Assets

	March 31, 2001	March 31, 2000
Current assets:		
Cash and cash equivalents	$ 109,251,426	$ 67,850,933
Short-term investments	2,000,000	15,760,000
Restricted investments	9,100,000	4,000,000
Receivables, net of allowance for doubtful accounts of $368,000 and $171,000 at March 31, 2001 and 2000, respectively	32,380,943	22,190,835
Maintenance deposits (note 5)	30,588,195	19,637,128
Prepaid expenses (note 2)	10,849,080	7,386,851
Inventories	4,072,335	2,235,183
Deferred tax asset (note 7)	1,506,218	1,136,194
Other current assets	45,621	163,527
Total current assets	199,793,818	140,360,651
Security, maintenance and other deposits (note 5)	45,680,373	17,613,122
Property and equipment, net (note 3)	38,100,126	21,654,262
Restricted investments	11,683,660	7,813,760
Other assets	58,621	104,243
	$ 295,316,598	$ 187,546,038

Liabilities and Stockholders' Equity

	March 31, 2001	March 31, 2000
Current liabilities:		
Accounts payable	$ 21,623,067	$ 14,407,913
Air traffic liability	62,663,237	44,518,837
Other accrued expenses (note 4)	18,236,479	17,542,019
Accrued maintenance expense (note 5)	33,510,531	21,893,316
Current portion of obligations under capital leases (note 5)	125,552	113,029
Total current liabilities	136,158,866	98,475,114
Accrued maintenance expense (note 5)	12,175,225	7,214,167
Deferred tax liability (note 7)	1,999,553	483,514
Obligations under capital leases, excluding current portion (note 5)	203,863	328,702
Total liabilities	150,537,507	106,501,497
Stockholders' equity:		
Preferred stock, no par value, authorized 1,000,000 shares; none issued		
Common stock, no par value, stated value of $.001 per share, authorized 40,000,000 shares; 28,194,602 and 26,598,410 shares issued and outstanding at March 31, 2001 and 2000, respectively	28,195	26,599
Additional paid-in capital	77,606,918	67,937,363
Unearned ESOP shares (note 10)	(1,662,087)	(857,713)
Retained earnings	68,806,065	13,938,292
Total stockholders' equity	144,779,091	81,044,541
	$ 295,316,598	$ 187,546,038

2

FRONTIER AIRLINES, INC. Statements of Income
Years Ended March 31, 2001, 2000, and 1999

	2001	2000	1999
Revenues:			
Passenger	$ 462,608,847	$ 320,850,271	$ 214,311,312
Cargo	7,516,867	6,855,882	4,881,066
Other	2,750,713	2,113,802	1,415,332
Total revenues	472,876,427	329,819,955	220,607,710
Operating expenses:			
Flight operations	179,453,300	125,536,174	79,247,347
Aircraft and traffic servicing	60,408,236	48,954,728	34,450,562
Maintenance	65,529,428	50,238,538	36,090,052
Promotion and sales	55,880,717	46,013,812	35,216,787
General and administrative	25,428,753	16,327,410	9,263,538
Depreciation and amortization	5,454,673	3,440,069	1,659,429
Total operating expenses	392,155,107	290,510,731	195,927,715
Operating income	80,721,320	39,309,224	24,679,995
Nonoperating income (expense):			
Interest income	7,897,282	4,334,688	1,556,047
Interest expense	(94,393)	(119,496)	(700,635)
Other, net	(191,771)	(109,798)	(448,917)
Total nonoperating income, net	7,611,118	4,105,394	406,495
Income before income tax expense (benefit) and cumulative effect of change in accounting principle	88,332,438	43,414,618	25,086,490
Income tax expense (benefit)	33,464,665	16,954,374	(5,479,570)
Income before cumulative effect of change in accounting principle	54,867,773	26,460,244	30,566,060
Cumulative effect of change in method of accounting for maintenance checks	-	549,009	-
Net income	$ 54,867,773	$ 27,009,253	$ 30,566,060

Section 1
Lease Accounting

LEASES DEFINED

A *lease* is a contract (agreement) calling for the *lessee* (user or tenant) to pay the *lessor* (owner or landlord) for the use of property. The lessee is obligated to make regular payments and takes possession of the asset from the lessor. Therefore, a lease is a way for a firm to finance the use of an asset. This section discusses the accounting for leases from the perspective of the lessee. Lease accounting by a lessor is covered in intermediate accounting.

THE DECISION TO LEASE VERSUS BUY

There are a number of factors that influence a firm's decision to lease versus buy an asset. Two important advantages of leasing are the minimal cash outlay upfront and the flexibility inherent in a lease. Both of these advantages are especially important in periods of rapid technological innovation. Leasing an asset for a short period of time allows firms to avoid technological obsolescence. Further, as firms expand and change their focus, they may not have cash readily available to purchase assets.

Certain industries use leasing more frequently than others. Typically, firms in capital-intensive industries, such as Verizon Communications, Alaska Airlines, and Office Depot, are heavy users of leases. Leases allow these firms to avoid the large capital outlay necessary to fund the underlying assets of the firm. Some leases also allow the firm to keep large amounts of assets and liabilities off the balance sheet. This chapter focuses on understanding accounting for the different types of leases and the effects this has on a firm's balance sheet.

TYPES OF LEASES

A lease is an *executory contract*—a mere exchange of promises. Under Generally Accepted Accounting Principles (GAAP), executory contracts do not create an asset or a liability until mutual performance occurs, that is, a transaction or exchange has taken place. There are specific accounting standards that require the obligations associated with certain types of leases to be recorded at lease inception even though the lease is an executory contract. Statement of Financial Accounting Standards (SFAS) No. 13 requires that a leased asset and the financial obligation associated with a lease be recognized on the balance sheet when the lease is economically equivalent to a purchase of an asset financed by a mortgage. For leases that represent the short-term use of another party's property (i.e., a rental), the lease is accounted for as an executory contract and a liability is recognized only as the rental period occurs.

4

Lessees classify leases into one of two types following the distinctions described above. A **capital lease** is recorded on the financial statements as the acquisition of an asset and an associated financing obligation because GAAP considers it to be economically equivalent to the financing of an asset purchase. An **operating lease** represents a short-term rental arrangement and is accounted for during each rental period.

Capital Leases

A lease that transfers the risks or benefits of ownership from the lessor to the lessee is economically equivalent to a financed purchase of the leased property. GAAP refers to these leases as *capital leases*. Accounting for a capital lease recognizes an asset (the item being leased) and a corresponding liability (for the present value of the required future lease payments) on the financial statements.

A cancelable lease does not transfer the risks and benefits of ownership. Thus, cancelable leases are not capital leases. For non-cancelable leases, SFAS No. 13 provides four objective criteria to determine if a lease is a capital lease. If a lease satisfies any <u>one</u> of the following four conditions, it is presumed that the lease transfers the risks or benefits of ownership and the lease is a capital lease.

Four conditions for capital lease accounting:

- the lease transfers ownership to the lessee at the end of the lease term; or

- the lease contains a "bargain purchase" option; or

- the lease extends for at least 75 percent of the asset's life; or

- the present value of the minimum contractual lease payments equals or exceeds 90 percent of the fair market value of the asset at the inception of the lease.

Each of these conditions attempts to determine whether there is a transfer of the risks and benefits of ownership.

Operating Leases

If the lease does not meet any of the four conditions above, then it does not transfer the risks or benefits of ownership from the lessor to the lessee. A firm does not recognize either the leased asset or the corresponding liability in its financial statements. *Operating leases* are a form of off-balance sheet financing (obligations to make payments in future periods that do not appear as a liability on the balance sheet).

A **CAPITAL LEASE** transfers the risks and rewards of ownership to the lessee, meets at least one of the four criteria established by GAAP, and results in the recording of an asset and liability on the lessee's books.

An **OPERATING LEASE** does not transfer the risks and rewards of ownership to the lessee, does not meet any of the four criteria established by GAAP, and as a result no asset or liability is recorded on the lessee's books.

INTERNATIONAL PERSPECTIVE:
Lease Accounting in Foreign Countries

International Accounting Standard (IAS) 17 is similar to SFAS 13 in that the substance of the lease transaction is more important than its legal form. IAS uses the term "financing lease" rather than capital lease. It calls for financing leases to be recorded on the balance sheet as assets and liabilities at amounts equal to the lesser of the fair value of the leased property or the present value of the minimum lease payments. The conditions that must be met to qualify as a financing lease are similar to those in US GAAP, although the language is less exact. For example, a lease is considered a financing lease if the lease term is for the *major part* of the economic life of the asset or if the present value of the minimum lease payments amounts to *at least substantially all* of the fair value of the leased asset. One requirement of IAS 17 that is different from US GAAP is that a lease is considered a financing lease if the leased assets are of a specialized nature such that only the lessee can use them without major modifications being made.

ACCOUNTING TREATMENT

We illustrate the accounting for leases using a simplified example. Assume that Frontier Airlines enters into a four-year lease for gate equipment on December 31, 2000. The lease requires Frontier to make annual payments of $16,462 at the end of each year. The firm's incremental borrowing rate is 12%. The present value of four payments of $16,462 at 12% is $50,000. The gate equipment has a fair market value of $70,000. The lease does not contain a bargain purchase option and the lease does not transfer ownership of the gate equipment to Frontier at the end of the lease.

Operating Lease Treatment

Assume that Frontier estimates the useful life of the gate equipment at eight years. The lease term of four years is only 50% of the asset's life. Thus, the lease does not meet the third criterion for capital lease treatment. There is no bargain purchase option or transfer of ownership so the lease does not meet the first two criteria. The present value of lease payments represents 71% of the fair market value of the asset, so the lease does not meet the fourth criterion. Frontier will account for the lease as an operating lease.

For an operating lease, no asset or liability is recorded at lease inception. Frontier will record only the lease payment and rent expense each period.

For 2001 through 2004, Frontier records the following journal entry[1]:

Rent expense (+E, -SE)	16,462	
Cash (-A)		16,462

Assets		=	Liabilities	+	Shareholders' Equity	
Cash	-16,462				Rent Expense	-16,462

Frontier must also disclose in the footnotes the amount of rent expense during all periods for which an income statement is presented, the minimum lease payments due in each of five years subsequent to the current period balance sheet date, and the lump sum of minimum lease payments due after five years.

Capital Lease Treatment

Assume that Frontier estimates the useful life of the gate equipment to be five years. The lease term of four years is 80% of the asset's life. Thus, the lease meets the third criterion for capital lease treatment, and Frontier will account for the lease as a capital lease.

Accounting for a capital lease is similar to accounting for a purchase of an asset financed with debt. The firm records an asset and liability at lease inception at the present value of the future minimum lease payments. The firm amortizes the leased asset and records the lease payment as a repayment of the lease obligation.

On December 31, 2000, Frontier records the following journal entry:

Leasehold (+A)	50,000	
Lease obligation (+L)		50,000

Assets		=	Liabilities		+	Shareholders' Equity
Leasehold	+50,000		Lease Obligation	+50,000		

A *leasehold* is the right of the lessee to use the leased property. Although a leasehold is an intangible asset, firms generally aggregate leaseholds with Property, Plant and Equipment on the balance sheet. A lease obligation is the present value of the contractual payments on the lease; it is a liability. This present value represents the amount that the lessee has borrowed from the lessor; it is the principal amount. The contractual lease payments repay this amount with interest. This concept is identical to the determination of the liability associated with a long-term debt or bond contract.

---

[1] If the cash payment date is not concurrent with Frontier's year end, Frontier would report either a rent payable liability or a prepaid rent asset.

The asset and liability are recorded at the present value of the future minimum lease payments unless the fair value of the leased asset at inception of the lease is lower. The lessee determines the present value of the future minimum lease payments using its *incremental borrowing rate* as the discount rate. The lessee's incremental borrowing rate is the rate at which it would borrow to buy the leased property at the inception of the lease. The lessee may use its rate on secured debt as its incremental borrowing rate.[2]

The **INCREMENTAL BORROWING RATE** is the interest rate the lessee would pay if it borrowed funds to buy the leased property at the inception of the lease.

Subsequent to lease inception, Frontier amortizes the asset (leasehold) and records payments of the liability (lease obligation). Most firms amortize leaseholds using the straight-line method. The amortization period is the useful life of the asset to the lessee, determined as a function of which criteria were met to qualify for capital lease accounting. If the lease qualifies as capital under either the 75% of useful life or 90% of fair value criteria, the amortization period is the length of the lease. The leasehold is completely amortized at the end of the lease, when the lessee no longer has use of the property. If the lease qualifies as capital under either the transfer of ownership or bargain purchase option criteria, the firm presumably will use the asset for its entire life, and accordingly, the amortization period is the estimated useful life of the asset. As with other intangible assets, amortization may be charged directly to the asset account rather than to a contra-asset account like "accumulated depreciation."

In 2001 through 2004, Frontier records annual amortization of $12,500 ($50,000/four years) as:

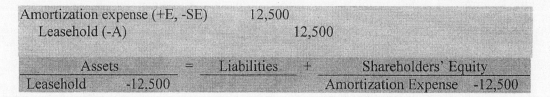

Amortization expense (+E, -SE)	12,500	
Leasehold (-A)		12,500

Assets	=	Liabilities	+	Shareholders' Equity
Leasehold -12,500				Amortization Expense -12,500

Frontier also records the annual lease payment. The lease payment is an allocation between interest and principal reduction of the lease obligation. Interest on the lease obligation is accounted for using the effective interest method. The interest expense for a period equals the product of the present value of the future lease payments and the discount rate assumed at inception of the lease. For 2001, for example, interest expense on the gate equipment lease is $6,000 ($50,000 x .12). The remainder of the 2001 payment of $10,462 is considered a reduction of the lease obligation.

Frontier records the following journal entry for the 2001 lease payment:

---

[2] If the fair value of the leasehold is less than the present value of the lease payments when they are calculated using the lessee's incremental borrowing rate, the lease is recorded at the asset's fair value. The lessor's implicit rate of return on the lease (computed based on the fair value) is the rate used to record subsequent lease payments.

```
2001:  Interest Expense (+E, -SE)        6,000
          Lease Obligation (-L)          10,462
                Cash (-A)                                    16,462
```

Assets		=	Liabilities		+	Shareholders' Equity	
Cash	-16,462		Lease Obligation	-10,462		Interest Expense	-6,000

Using this method, the lease obligation will reduce to zero as of the end of the lease term, and at any point during the course of the lease, the lease obligation will equal the present value of the *remaining* lease payments.

In 2002, the lease payment continues to be recorded using the effective interest method, but the allocation between interest and principal reduction changes. The calculation of interest is based on the amount of the outstanding lease obligation, which was reduced by $10,462 in 2001. Thus, the outstanding lease obligation for 2002 is $39,538 ($50,000 - $10,462), which represents the present value of the remaining three lease payments discounted at 12%. Interest expense for 2002 is $4,745 ($39,538 x .12). The journal entry Frontier records for 2002 is:

```
2002:  Interest Expense (+E, -SE)        4,745
          Lease Obligation (-L)          11,717
                Cash (-A)                                    16,462
```

Assets		=	Liabilities		+	Shareholders' Equity	
Cash	-16,462		Lease Obligation	-11,717		Interest Expense	-4,745

The final two journal entries are shown below.

```
2003:  Interest Expense (+E, -SE)        3,339
          Lease Obligation (-L)          13,123
                Cash (-A)                                    16,462

       [Interest expense = $27,821 x .12 = $3,339]
```

Assets		=	Liabilities		+	Shareholders' Equity	
Cash	-16,462		Lease Obligation	-13,123		Interest Expense	-3,339

```
2004:  Interest Expense (+E, -SE)        1,764
          Lease Obligation (-L)          14,698
                Cash (-A)                                    16,462

       [Interest expense = $14,698 x .12 = $1,764]
```

Assets		=	Liabilities		+	Shareholders' Equity	
Cash	-16,462		Lease Obligation	-14,698		Interest Expense	-1,764

The leasehold obligation is zero at the end of the four-year lease term ($50,000 - $10,462 - $11,717 - $13,123 - $14,698 = 0). Total cash paid is $65,848, of which $50,000 represents principal reduction and $15,848 represents interest.

For capital leases, Frontier must also disclose the minimum lease payments due in each of five years subsequent to the current period balance sheet date and the lump sum of minimum lease payments due after five years. Firms must also report the present value of the minimum lease payments and the portion of the total lease payments allocated to interest.

REAL WORLD EXCERPT:
FRONTIER AIRLINES
Annual Report

(5) Lease Commitments (excerpt)

Minimum future lease payments on non-cancelable leases at March 31, 2001 are as follows:

	Capital Leases	Operating Leases
	(In thousands)	
2002	$ 153,320	$ 73,686,103
2003	153,320	76,398,616
2004	44,322	77,206,098
2005	-	69,403,130
2006	-	53,539,139
Thereafter	-	413,585,032
Total minimum lease payments	$350,962	$763,818,118
Less interest	21,547	
Capital lease obligations	$329,415	
Less current portion	125,552	
Long-term capital lease obligations	$203,863	

The obligations under capital leases have been discounted at imputed interest rates ranging from 10% to 13%.

Rental expense under operating leases, including month-to-month leases, for the years ended March 31, 2001, 2000, and 1999 was $80,781,897, $65,201,876 and $46,099,140, respectively.

10

At March 31, 2001, Frontier's balance sheet reports $329,415 in capital lease obligations, of which $125,552 is current. The lease footnote shows that Frontier has operating leases in addition to the capital leases reflected on the balance sheet. For both capital and operating leases, Frontier reports the subsequent five years of minimum lease payments and a lump sum of payments to be made after five years. For capital leases, Frontier shows the calculation of the present value of the lease obligation. The present value is the difference between the total cash payments and the portion that represents interest. Frontier further reports the breakdown between current and long-term obligations, which corresponds to the presentation on the balance sheet.

FINANCIAL STATEMENT EFFECTS OF OPERATING VERSUS CAPITAL LEASES

Balance Sheet

Firms do not record an asset or a liability for an operating lease. Thus, all else equal, a firm that uses operating leases will have lower assets and lower liabilities than if it were to use capital leases.

The effect on the balance sheet is illustrated below using the Frontier Airlines simplified example. Assets and liabilities are considerably higher when the firm classifies the gate equipment lease as capital rather than operating. Note that the asset and liability decrease at different rates over the four years, but both have values of zero at the end of the lease term.

December 31:	2000	2001	2002	2003	2004
Operating lease:					
Asset	$ 0	$ 0	$ 0	$ 0	$ 0
Liability	0	0	0	0	0
Capital lease:					
Asset	50,000	37,500	25,000	12,500	0
Liability	50,000	39,538	27,821	14,698	0

Income Statement

Firms recognize rent expense on operating leases equal to the lease payments associated with the period. For capital leases, two charges affect the income statement: amortization expense and interest expense. How does the sum of amortization expense and interest expense compare to rent expense? Over the life of the lease, total rent expense equals the sum of total amortization expense and interest expense as shown below using the Frontier Airlines gate equipment example.

Year ended December 31:	2001	2002	2003	2004	Total
Operating lease:					
Rent expense	$ 16,462	$ 16,462	$ 16,462	$ 16,462	$ 65,848
Capital lease:					
Interest expense	$ 6,000	$ 4,745	$ 3,339	$ 1,764	$ 15,848
Amortization expense	12,500	12,500	12,500	12,500	50,000
Total	$ 18,500	$ 17,245	$ 15,839	$ 14,264	$ 65,848

Over the life of an operating lease, total lease payments equal total rent. Over the life of a capital lease, total lease payments equal total interest expense plus the initial lease obligation. This is evident in the journal entries associated with the lease payments. In our example, total lease payments equal $65,848. Note that the initial lease obligation equals the initial value of the leasehold asset. Because the leasehold asset is amortized to zero, total amortization expense equals the amount of the lease obligation at lease inception. Hence, total amortization expense plus total interest expense equals total lease payments, which is the sum of rent expense under operating lease accounting. The table above illustrates this relation.

Although the total charged to expense over the life of the lease is the same whether a firm classifies a lease as operating or capital, the classification affects the period in which the expense is recognized. Rent expense is typically constant over the lease term. Amortization expense is also constant because firms normally use the straight-line method. However, interest expense is higher in the early years of the lease due to the use of the effective interest method. Thus, the sum of amortization and interest expense is typically greater than rent expense in the early years of the lease term, but less than rent expense in the later years. This effect is accentuated if the firm uses an accelerated amortization method for the asset.

Return to the Frontier Airlines example. Total expenses assuming the lease is a capital lease are greater than total expenses assuming the lease is an operating lease in 2001 and 2002. This relation reverses in 2003 and 2004. Total expenses over the life of the lease are $65,848 whether the lease is accounted for as an operating lease or a capital lease. The accounting method does not change the fact that the cost of the lease is $65,848 over four years.

Now that we have examined the impact of capital lease accounting on the balance sheet and the income statement, we can understand the dramatic impact that lease classification can have on a firm's ratios. Consider the debt-to-equity ratio. A firm that is a heavy user of leases will have higher liabilities if it accounts for those leases as capital leases rather than operating leases. Equity, which includes retained earnings, will be largely unaffected. Thus, a firm that uses capital leases will have a higher debt-to-equity ratio than a firm that uses operating leases.

12

Statement of Cash Flows
The accounting treatment of the lease does not affect total cash flows. However, capital lease and operating lease treatment affect cash flow classification within the Statement of Cash Flows.

For an operating lease, the lease payment is an operating cash outflow because renting is an operating activity. For a capital lease, the interest portion of the payment is an operating cash outflow, but the portion associated with the reduction of the lease obligation is a financing cash outflow.

Thus, all else equal, operating lease classification results in lower operating cash flows as reported on the statement of cash flows than capital lease classification. Capital lease classification results in lower financing cash flows. It is important to note that these results are merely a classification issue; total cash flow is *unaffected* by lease accounting.

We use the Frontier Airlines simplified example to illustrate the effect of operating versus capital lease classification on the statement of cash flows for fiscal year 2001. Frontier's total cash payment in 2001 is $16,462 regardless of whether the lease is accounted for as an operating or capital lease. Using operating lease accounting, this cash payment reduces operating cash flow by $16,462 because it is considered rent expense. Using capital lease accounting, the payment consists of $6,000 in interest expense and $10,462 in principal reduction. The payment reduces operating cash flow by $6,000 because interest is an operating activity and reduces financing cash flow by $10,462 because the reduction in the lease obligation is a financing activity. Thus, when the lease is classified as operating, Frontier's operating cash flow is $10,462 lower than if it had classified the lease as a capital lease. However, its financing cash flow is $10,462 higher.

FINANCIAL ANALYSIS: CAPITALIZING OPERATING LEASES

Purpose of Capitalizing Operating Leases
Non-cancelable leases meet two of the three criteria for an obligation to be recorded as a liability on the balance sheet: there is a probable future sacrifice of economic resources and the firm has little or no discretion to avoid the transfer. Whether a lease is classified as operating or capital under GAAP, the lessee still has an obligation to pay the lessor and benefits from the use of the asset. The obligation associated with operating leases is not on the balance sheet. Thus, an analyst can get a better picture of a firm's obligations by "recording" a liability and an asset associated with operating leases even though GAAP does not require this treatment. The process of recasting the financial statements to reflect the obligations of operating leases and the associated assets is called "capitalizing operating leases."

One could argue that operating leases should not be considered an obligation, as are capital leases. The GAAP criteria that differentiate operating leases from capital leases are intended to distinguish leases that are economically equivalent to short-term rentals from long-term financings. However, the specific numerical thresholds in the lease classification criteria allow firms to structure leases that are "almost" financing transactions but do not meet the requirements for capital lease accounting. For example, a firm can structure a lease with a term that represents 74% of the asset's useful life and payments that equal 89% of the fair market value of the asset. As a result of these "bright line" rules, some economically similar transactions are accounted for by very different methods.

In summary, the process of capitalizing operating leases presents a more conservative view of the financial position of the firm and often better reflects the economic realities of the firm.

Steps to capitalizing operating leases

To capitalize a firm's operating leases, one must determine the amount of the liability and the leasehold asset that would be on the firm's balance sheet if the leases had initially been recorded as capital leases. The analyst uses these amounts to adjust the income statement and statement of cash flows to reflect lease capitalization. Adjusting the income statement, however, is of secondary importance. As illustrated previously, the effects of capital lease treatment versus operating lease treatment are most significant for the balance sheet and are typically relatively insignificant for the income statement.

Step 1: Calculate the present value of the minimum operating lease payments at the current balance sheet date. This calculation requires two assumptions:

The discount rate: The appropriate discount rate is the lessee's incremental borrowing rate for debt with risk similar to the lease. If a firm has capital leases in addition to the operating leases that are being capitalized, the discount rate associated with the capital leases is a reasonable proxy for the appropriate discount rate. Firms disclose this rate, or information necessary to calculate this rate, in the lease footnote. If a firm does not have capital leases, one can estimate an appropriate discount rate using information about the firm's long-term debt.

14

The future minimum lease payments: Firms report the minimum lease payments for the five years after the balance sheet date in the footnotes. Payments for subsequent years are reported only in the aggregate. In order to compute the present value of the "lump sum" flow, one must make an assumption about the timing of the aggregate payments. Some common assumptions are:

    i) annual payments will continue at the same rate as in year five,

    ii) all payments are made in year six, or

    iii) payments decrease according to the pattern in years one through five.

Step 2: Adjust the balance sheet to reflect the leasehold asset and lease obligation.

Add the present value of the minimum operating lease payments to both long-term assets and long-term debt. This procedure provides a relatively accurate representation of the firm's lease obligation. If the operating leases had been accounted for as capital leases since inception, the liability at any point in time equals the present value of the future payments. However, this procedure does not provide an accurate representation of the leasehold asset that would appear on the balance sheet if the operating leases had been accounted for as capital leases since inception. The leasehold asset is unlikely to equal the lease obligation at any date subsequent to lease inception because firms typically record amortization on a straight-line basis while principal is reduced using the effective interest method. Because the capitalization of operating leases focuses on liabilities, this method is common.

Step 3: Adjust the income statement for amortization and interest expense.

Determine amortization expense on the "asset" (assume the amortization period) and interest expense on the "debt" (using the same discount rate as above).[3] Remove rent expense from the income statement.

---

[3] Interest expense calculated on the amount of the liability at the **end** of the year is actually interest expense for the **next** year. Some analysts use this as an estimate of the current year's interest because the calculation is easier and interest expense from one year to the next is not economically different. The difference is larger the shorter the term of the debt.

Step 4: Adjust the statement of cash flows for the classification difference between lease payments of operating versus capital leases.

Determine the portion of the lease payment that represents a repayment of the liability and reclassify it from an operating cash outflow to a financing cash outflow.

Steps 3 and 4 are not as critical to an analysis as steps 1 and 2 because most analysts want to understand the amount of future obligations associated with lease payments. Furthermore, the balance sheet adjustment is typically the most significant in magnitude.

FOCUS COMPANY ANALYSIS: Capitalizing Operating Leases FRONTIER AIRLINES

Step 1. Calculate the present value of minimum operating lease payments as of March 31, 2001.

The lease footnote provides the subsequent five years' minimum lease payments and one "thereafter" payment. We must assume the timing of the payments within the lump sum of $413,585,032. Assuming that payments after 2006 continue at approximately the same level as in 2006, the lump sum is equivalent to 7.73 payments. Rounding this to eight payments (to simplify the present value calculation) results in an eight-year annuity of $51,698,129.

The most appropriate discount rate to use as a proxy for the lessee's incremental borrowing rate is the discount rate implied by the firm's capital lease obligations. The footnote reports that imputed rates range from 10% to 13%. These rates can be calibrated with information from the firm's long-term debt footnote. Recall that the incremental borrowing rate should represent the rate on debt of similar risk. Using data in Frontier's debt footnote (not reported), we choose a discount rate of 10%.

The present value of the five minimum payments through 2006 at 10% plus the present value of the eight-year annuity of $51,698,129 at 10% is $440,033,309.

16

Step 2. Increase Frontier's assets and liabilities by the present value of minimum operating lease payments.

The increase of $440,033,309 represents a 149% increase in total assets and a 292% increase in total liabilities. The KEY ratio analysis below demonstrates the effect of this change on the debt to equity ratio – a primary measure of solvency.

Step 3. Adjust the income statement.

Use the asset and liability value of $440,033,309 to estimate amortization and interest expense for the year ended March 31, 2001. The resulting estimates actually represent amortization and interest expense for the year ended March 31, 2002. For simplicity, however, we assume amortization and interest will not change dramatically from one year to the next.

Amortization Expense = $440,033,309/13 = $33,848,716
    (The 13-year lease life equals the first five years of payments plus the eight year annuity assumed for the "thereafter" payment.)
Interest Expense = $440,033,309 x .10 = $44,003,331
(The interest rate of 10% is the discount rate used to compute the present value.)

Eliminate rent expense of $80,781,897 for the year ended March 31, 2001 (as reported in the lease footnote).

In total, increase pretax income by $2,929,850, which is rent expense less the sum of amortization expense and interest expense {$80,781,897 – ($33,848,716 + $44,003,331)}. This amount is a 3.3 percent increase over reported pre-tax income and demonstrates that the effect of capitalizing operating leases on the income statement is trivial relative to the effect on the balance sheet.

Step 4. Adjust the statement of cash flows. Reclassify the reduction in the lease liability from an operating cash outflow to a financing cash outflow.

The difference between the lease payment and interest expense represents the reduction in the lease obligation. For the year ended March 31, 2001, the reduction in the lease obligation would have been $36,778,566 (80,781,897 – 44,003,331). Thus, financing cash flow is reduced and operating cash flow is increased by $36,778,566. Total cash flow remains unchanged.

KEY RATIO ANALYSIS: Debt to Equity Ratio

ANALYTICAL QUESTION

What is the effect on the firm of capitalizing operating leases? Will this affect our assessment of the firm's solvency?

Debt to Equity = (Total Debt + Capitalized Operating Leases) ÷ Total Equity

RATIO AND COMPARISONS

Comparison before and after the adjustment:

Before: After:

$$\frac{150,537,507}{144,779,091}$$ $$\frac{(150,537,507 + 440,033,309)}{144,779,091}$$

= 1.04   = 4.08

INTERPRETATIONS

When making comparisons across firms using adjusted numbers, it is important to make similar adjustments across all firms. It is also useful to do a sensitivity analysis. In other words, how sensitive is the revised Debt to Equity ratio of 4.08 to our assumption of a discount rate of 10% or an eight year annuity after 2006?

Note that we did not adjust equity because, typically, the most significant effect of operating lease accounting is that liabilities are kept off the balance sheet. However, the assumption that the impact on equity is immaterial is less reasonable in the early stages of the lease and the shorter the lease term.

Obviously Frontier uses operating leases as a primary source of financing. To neglect the obligation (and asset) associated with these leases would be to neglect the firm's primary business mission. Without these leased aircraft, Frontier Airlines would cease to exist.

CHAPTER TAKE-AWAYS

1. **Understand the differences between capital and operating of leases.**
   Capital leases are those that transfer the risks and benefits of ownership from the lessor to the lessee. Operating leases are those that do not transfer the risks and benefits of ownership to the lessee. A lease that satisfies one of GAAP's four conditions for determining whether a lease transfers the risks and benefits of ownership is treated as a capital lease.

2. **Understand the financial statement effects of operating versus capital lease accounting.**
   Operating lease accounting only recognizes periodic rent expense. The firm does not record an asset or liability. Capital lease accounting mirrors that of a purchase of equipment with long-term debt. The firm recognizes an asset and liability and the related periodic interest and amortization expense. The recognition of the asset and liability can have a significant impact on the balance sheet. The effects on the income statement are much less significant. Lease payments on operating leases are considered rent expense. Firms with capital leases report amortization expense and interest expense. In the early part of the lease term, rent expense is typically lower than the sum of amortization and interest, but it is higher in the latter part of the lease term. Because it reflects the activity "renting", the lease payment is an operating cash outflow for operating leases. The lease payment is recorded as interest expense (an operating cash outflow) and principal reduction (a financing cash outflow) under capital lease accounting.

3. **Capitalize operating leases.**
   Operating leases are a form of off-balance sheet financing. One can adjust a firm's financial statements to reflect the additional obligation by capitalizing operating leases. This adjustment provides a more accurate picture of the firm's financing obligations.

EXERCISES

E1-1 Classifying Leases

New Mexico Valve (NMV) has an incremental borrowing rate of 12%. NMV has entered into the following leases:

Lease 1 – NMV leases a color copy machine for three years with annual payments of $2,100 at the end of each year. At the end of the lease, NMV may return the copy machine to the lessor or purchase the copy machine for $1,700. NMV estimates that the copy machine has a useful life of five years and will be worth approximately $1,400 at the expiration of the lease. A comparable copy machine currently sells for $5,500.

Lease 2 – Due to increasing sales, NMV decides to open an additional sales office in a neighboring city. NMV has the option to purchase the building and land for $220,000. NMV estimates that the land represents approximately 25% of market value. While the building will be useable for the next 20 years, NMV is still uncertain about the prospects of the new sales office and therefore opts for a two-year lease. NMV must pay $2,000 upfront and $2,000 at the end of each quarter.

Lease 3 – In order to furnish its new office building, NMV leases $15,000 of office equipment. NMV pays a fee of $275 per week for the equipment. NMV may cancel the lease with two weeks notice.

Lease 4 – In order to implement Just-In-Time inventory management, NMV leases a server, 12 workstations and inventory management software for four years. At the end of the lease, NMV will own the equipment and software, but the Information Systems department expects the hardware and software to be obsolete.

Required:

Determine whether each lease is an operating or a capital lease and explain the reason(s) for the classification.

E1-2 Classifying and Recording Leases

On January 1, 2003, Bay State Delivery (BSD) leases a truck for three years. The lease is noncancelable by either party. The annual lease payment on the contract is $14,074, due at the end of each year. Assume that the fair value of the truck is $40,000; it has a three-year life and zero salvage value. BSD has an incremental borrowing rate of 10 percent and closes its books on December 31 of each year.

Required:
1. Should BSD account for this lease as a capital lease or an operating lease?
2. Prepare dated journal entries for the lease assuming that BSD leases the truck for three years.

E1-3 Classifying and Recording Leases

Refer to the facts of problem E1-2 above, but now assume that the truck has a useful life of five years.

Required:
1. Should BSD account for this lease as a capital lease or an operating lease?
2. Prepare dated journal entries for the lease assuming that the truck has a useful life of five years.

E1-4 Effect of Using Different Interest Rates

Exterior Dimension Inc. (EDI) produces aluminum siding for commercial applications. At the beginning of the fiscal year, EDI leases four lift-trucks to use in its warehouse facility. The lease terms are six years, and the leases contain bargain purchase options. Currently, the firm has short-term unsecured debt on which it pays an annual rate of 11 percent. The firm also has long-term secured debt that carries an annual rate of 8 percent. EDI doesn't know whether to define its incremental borrowing rate as 11% or 8%.

Required:
1. What is the effect (i.e., increase, decrease, remains the same) of choosing 11% rather than 8% on the following items in the first year of operations?
   a. Total Liabilities
   b. Amortization Expense on Leasehold Assets
   c. Cash
2. Which interest rate should EDI use? Why?

E1-5 Cash Flow Impact of Lease Classification

At the beginning of year one, Bakers Express leases a delivery truck for five years. Bakers Express will make annual lease payments of $6,000, due at the end of each year. Bakers Express has an incremental borrowing rate of 15 percent.

Required:

1. If Bakers Express accounts for the lease as an operating lease, what is the impact on total cash flow in year one? What is the impact on operating, investing and financing cash flow in year one?
2. If Bakers Express accounts for the lease as a capital lease, what is the impact on total cash flow in year one? What is the impact on operating, investing and financing cash flow in year one?

E1-6 Determining Financial Statement Effects

The WolverFrog Company is a manufacturer of high quality steamrollers. WolverFrog enters into long-term leases related to plant and equipment. These leases qualify as operating leases. For each of the following items, indicate the effect (i.e., higher, lower or remains the same) of accounting for these leases as operating rather than capital leases in the first year of operations. Assume straight-line depreciation.

1. Property, Plant and Equipment
2. Long-term Liabilities
3. Current Liabilities
4. Net Income
5. Cash
6. Operating Cash Flow
7. Debt to Equity Ratio

PROBLEMS

P1-1 Calculating Interest Expense and Amortization Expense

The Gripe Corporation has a single capital lease that was signed on January 1, 2001. Gripe's incremental borrowing rate is 12 percent. The lease term is 10 years, and Gripe will return the leased asset to the lessor at the end of 10 years. Gripe's December 31, 2002, balance sheet shows the following information:

Leased Asset (Net) $54,000

Amortization is calculated using the straight-line method. Assume that Gripe makes the lease payments on the last day of each year.

Required:
1. Calculate interest expense and amortization expense for the first two years of the lease and give the corresponding journal entries.
2. Calculate the value of the assets and liabilities related to the lease that appeared on Gripe's balance sheet at the end of 2001 and 2002.

P1-2 Lease Classification Effects on Ratios

Industrial Innovations Corp. decides to expand operations, which requires that the company increase its available warehouse space. Industrial Innovation's real estate broker identifies an appropriate building. The owner is willing to provide two different lease options. The warehouse has a useful life of 15 years and a fair value of $145,000. Neither lease alternative transfers ownership nor contains a purchase option.

Option 1 – A ten-year lease with annual lease payments of $25,000 due at the end of each year.

Option 2 – An eight-year lease with annual lease payments of $27,000 due at the end of each year.

The company records show the following related amounts (prior to the effect of the lease):

Total Assets	$176,000
Total Liabilities	98,000
Total Equity	78,000

Industrial Innovations has an incremental borrowing rate of 13% and has an agreement with its creditors to maintain a debt to equity ratio below 1.5.

Required:
1. Calculate the new debt to equity ratio at lease inception under option 1.
2. Calculate the new debt to equity ratio at lease inception under option 2.
3. Why would Industrial Innovations prefer option 1? option 2? Which option do you think they will choose?

CASES AND PROJECTS

C1-1 Capital Versus Operating Leases

Refer to excerpts from the financial statements and footnotes of Wal-Mart Stores Incorporated below and on the following pages.

Required:

1. What is the minimum amount of rent expense that Wal-Mart will include in the income statement for fiscal 2003 (i.e., year ended January 31, 2003) relating to leases in place at January 31, 2002?

2. Approximate the total expense recorded by Wal-Mart during fiscal 2002 relating to capital leases. Assume that all property under capital leases relates to 20-year leases. Further assume that any new capital leases and terminations were effective on the first day of the fiscal year.

3. If the capital leases were instead treated as operating leases, what would be the amount of total expense recorded for the period? Assume that all interest costs relating to lease obligations are paid as incurred.

4. Capitalize the operating leases as of January 31, 2002. Assume that Wal-Mart has an incremental borrowing rate of 10% and that the payments after 2007 are made in equal installments of $570 million for nine consecutive years.

5. Calculate the debt to equity ratio and the debt to total assets ratio as reported by Wal-mart before and after capitalizing the operating leases. Define debt as the sum of commercial paper, obligations under capital leases and long-term debt including the current portions, and define equity as "Total Shareholders Equity".

25

WAL MART STORES INC

Note 9. Commitments and Contingencies

The Company and certain of its subsidiaries have long-term leases for stores and equipment. Rentals (including, for certain leases, amounts applicable to taxes, insurance, maintenance, other operating expenses and contingent rentals) under all operating leases were $1,043 million, $893 million, and $762 million in 2002, 2001, and 2000, respectively. Aggregate minimum annual rentals at January 31, 2002, under non-cancelable leases are as follows (in millions):

Fiscal year	Operating leases	Capital leases
2003	$ 623	$ 425
2004	602	424
2005	586	423
2006	565	419
2007	547	409
Thereafter	5,131	3,414
Total minimum rentals	$ 8,054	5,514
Less estimated executory costs		63
Net minimum lease payments		5,451
Less imputed interest at rates ranging from 6.1% to14.0%		2,258
Present value of minimum lease payments		$ 3,193

WAL MART STORES INC
Consolidated Balance Sheets
(Amounts in millions)
January 31,

	2002	2001
Assets		
Current Assets		
.		
.		
.		
Total Current Assets	28,246	26,555
Property, Plant and Equipment, at Cost		
.		
.		
.		
Net property, plant and equipment	42,556	37,617
Property Under Capital Lease		
Property under capital lease	4,626	4,620
Less accumulated amortization	1,432	1,303
Net property under capital leases	3,194	3,317
Other Assets and Deferred Charges		
Net goodwill and other acquired intangible assets	8,595	9,059
Other assets and deferred charges	860	1,582
Total Assets	$ 83,451	$ 78,130
Liabilities and Shareholders Equity		
Current Liabilities		
Commercial paper	$ 743	$ 2,286
Accounts payable	15,617	15,092
Accrued liabilities	7,174	6,355
Accrued income taxes	1,343	841
Long-term debt due within one year	2,257	4,234
Obligations under capital leases due within one year	148	141
Total Current Liabilities	27,282	28,949
Long-Term Debt	15,687	12,501
Long-Term Obligations Under Capital Leases	3,045	3,154
Deferred Income Taxes and Other	1,128	1,043
Minority Interest	1,207	1,140
Shareholders Equity		
Preferred stock ($0.10 par value; 100 shares authorized, none issued)		
Common stock ($0.10 par value; 11,000 shares authorized, 4,453 and 4,470 issued and outstanding in 2002 and 2001, respectively)	445	447
Capital in excess of par value	1,484	1,411
Retained earnings	34,441	30,169
Other accumulated comprehensive income	(1,268)	(684)
Total Shareholders Equity	35,102	31,343
Total Liabilities and Shareholders Equity	$ 83,451	$ 78,130

WAL MART STORES INC
Consolidated Statements of Income
(Amounts in millions except per share data)
Fiscal years ended January 31,

	2002	2001	2000
Revenues			
Net sales	$ 217,799	$ 191,329	$ 165,013
Other income-net	2,013	1,966	1,796
	219,812	193,295	166,809
Costs and Expenses			
Cost of sales	171,562	150,255	129,664
Operating, selling and general and administrative expenses	36,173	31,550	27,040
Interest Costs			
Debt	1,052	1,095	756
Capital leases	274	279	266
	209,061	183,179	157,726
Income Before Income Taxes, Minority Interest and Cumulative Effect of Accounting Change	10,751	10,116	9,083
Provision for Income Taxes			
Current	3,712	3,350	3,476
Deferred	185	342	(138)
	3,897	3,692	3,338
Income Before Minority Interest and Cumulative Effect of Accounting Change	6,854	6,424	5,745
Minority Interest	(183)	(129)	(170)
Income Before Cumulative Effect of Accounting Change	6,671	6,295	5,575
Cumulative Effect of Accounting Change, net of tax benefit of $119			(198)
Net Income	$ 6,671	$ 6,295	$ 5,377

WAL MART STORES INC
Consolidated Statements of Cash Flows
(Amounts in millions)

Fiscal years ended January 31,	2002	2001	2000
Cash flows from operating activities			
Net Income	$ 6,671	$ 6,295	$ 5,377
Net cash provided by operating activities	10,260	9,604	8,194
Cash flows from investing activities			
Net cash used in investing activities	(7,146)	(8,714)	(16,846)
Cash flows from financing activities			
Increase/(decrease) in commercial paper	(1,533)	(2,022)	4,316
Proceeds from issuance of long-term debt	4,591	3,778	6,000
Purchase of Company stock	(1,214)	(193)	(101)
Dividends paid	(1,249)	(1,070)	(890)
Payment of long-term debt	(3,519)	(1,519)	(863)
Payment of capital lease obligations	(167)	(173)	(133)
Proceeds from issuance of Company stock		581	
Other financing activities	113	176	224
Net cash provided by (used in) financing activities	(2,978)	(442)	8,553
Effect of exchange rate changes on cash	(29)	(250)	76
Net increase/(decrease) in cash and cash equivalents	107	198	(23)
Cash and cash equivalents at beginning of year	2,054	1,856	1,879
Cash and cash equivalents at end of year	$ 2,161	$ 2,054	$ 1,856

C1-2 Capitalizing Operating Leases

Refer to the excerpts from Dover Corporation's 2001 Annual Report on the following page.

Required:

1. Discount the future minimum lease payments (MLPs), assuming that Dover's incremental borrowing rate is 7%, any payments made after 2006 are paid in 2006, and the average remaining useful life of the lease assets is five years.
2. Had Dover classified these operating leases as capital leases, what would have been the effect on assets, liabilities and operating income as of December 31, 2001?
3. What would have been the effect on Dover's debt to equity ratio? Define debt as the sum of notes payable and long-term debt including the current portion, and define equity as "Net Stockholder's Equity".

4. Qualitatively discuss the impact of classifying these leases as operating rather than capital on Dover's Statement of Cash Flow. Discuss the effect on operating, investing and financing as well as total cash flows.

DOVER CORPORATION AND SUBSIDIARIES
Excerpt from Footnotes to the financial statements:

Note 11. Rental and Lease Information

The Company leases certain facilities and equipment under operating leases, many of which contain renewal options. Total rental expense, net of insignificant sublease rental income, on all operating leases was $43,119,000, $34,810,000, and $31,520,000 for 2001, 2000, and 1999, respectively. Contingent rentals under the operating leases were not significant.

Minimum future rental commitments under operating leases having noncancelable lease terms in excess of one year aggregate $151 million as of December 31, 2001, and are payable as follows (in millions): 2002 - $33; 2003 - $25; 2004 - $19; 2005 - $16; and in 2006 and subsequent years - $58.

DOVER CORPORATION AND SUBSIDIARIES
CONSOLIDATED BALANCE SHEETS
(in thousands, except share and per share figures)

December 31,	2001	2000
Assets		
Current Assets:		
Total current assets	1,654,928	1,908,674
Property, plant and equipment, at cost:		
Land	44,174	44,307
Buildings	416,995	367,565
Machinery and equipment	1,295,046	1,174,014
	1,756,215	1,585,886
Less accumulated depreciation	994,854	870,642
Net property, plant and equipment	761,361	715,244
Goodwill, net of amortization	1,946,423	1,793,556
Intangible assets, net of amortization	173,194	179,510
Other assets and deferred charges	56,359	82,883
Assets from discontinued operations	9,937	213,896
	$ 4,602,202	$ 4,893,763
Liabilities		
Current Liabilities:		
Notes payable	$ 39,783	$ 839,880
Current maturities of long-term debt	3,997	2,657
Accounts payable	207,295	266,729
Accrued compensation and employee benefits	156,135	173,011
Accrued insurance	45,602	45,532
Other accrued expenses	211,060	198,183
Federal and other taxes on income	155,299	43,535
Total current liabilities	819,171	1,569,527
Long-term debt	1,033,243	631,846
Deferred income taxes	102,853	67,760
Other deferrals (principally compensation)	107,555	145,102
Liabilities from discontinued operations	19,841	37,953
Commitments and contingent liabilities		
Shareholders Equity		
Net stockholders equity	2,519,539	2,441,575

Section 2
Income Taxes

Frontier reports tax expense in the income statement of its annual report based on financial accounting rules, but completes its tax return using a different set of accounting rules. This practice is perfectly legal and is shared by all large companies. In this section of the supplement, we discuss why corporations follow this accounting practice and describe its implications.

Like the treatment of all other costs, income taxes are accounted for in the financial statements based on the accrual method. Firms do not expense the income taxes that they pay for a current year. Firms expense the taxes that are associated with their current period income as measured by GAAP. Taxes paid and taxes associated with financial reporting (GAAP) income can differ substantially. The result is significant tax-related assets and liabilities that represent taxes paid in advance of being expensed or accruals of taxes to be paid in later periods.

In the United States, firms report and pay income taxes quarterly to the Internal Revenue Service, which monitors forms and payments. Although this chapter discusses income taxes under the U.S. system, the accounting for income taxes and the resulting appearance of the financial statements applies to any accounting system with separate tax and financial reporting rules. The Internal Revenue Code (IRC) is complex. In this chapter, we simplify the discussion of the IRC rules and the tax treatment of particular transactions. The focus of the chapter is on the GAAP treatment of income taxes in the financial statements.

Taxable income versus GAAP pre-tax income

Firms report *taxable income* to tax authorities based on the Internal Revenue Code (IRC), which establishes rules for calculating taxable revenues and tax deductible expenses. These rules differ from the GAAP rules for recognizing revenues and expenses. Thus, taxable income is not equivalent to pretax income reported in the financial statements as measured under GAAP. Income taxes are a function of taxable income; tax expense is a function of GAAP pretax income. The fact that revenue and expense recognition rules are different under GAAP and under the IRC makes sense given the different objectives of the financial reporting system and the U.S. tax system.

TAXABLE INCOME is income calculated using the rules established by the Internal Revenue Code, and is not the same as GAAP pre-tax net income.

The difference between GAAP and IRC revenue and expense recognition rules result in differences between the tax basis and the GAAP basis of a firm's assets and liabilities. Every revenue or expense is associated with an asset or liability account. For example, depreciation expense represents the allocation of the cost of property, plant and equipment. Sales revenue is accrued as an account receivable until received in cash. If depreciation expense or sales revenue are recognized differently under GAAP and the IRC rules, then the related accounts – Property, Plant and Equipment (PP&E) and accounts receivable – will be different for GAAP and IRC purposes.

The differences between GAAP pretax income and IRC taxable income can be classified into two categories, temporary differences and permanent differences.

Temporary differences

Some transactions or activities lead to *temporary differences* between GAAP pretax income and IRC taxable income. The differences are temporary in that the firm will recognize the same amount of revenue or expense for GAAP and IRC purposes in total over the life of the associated asset or liability. However, the GAAP revenue or expense will be recognized in different periods than the IRC revenue or expense. In any given year, GAAP pretax income and IRC taxable income related to the transaction will differ. The GAAP basis, which is its value according to GAAP rules, and the IRC basis, which is its value according to the IRC rules, of the related asset (or liability) will also be different during its life, but the bases will eventually be the same when the asset (or liability) is consumed or paid.[1]

Depreciation of property, plant, and equipment (PP&E) is an example of an activity that leads to a temporary difference between GAAP pretax income and taxable income and between the GAAP basis and the tax basis of a firm's assets. For tax purposes, firms depreciate depreciable assets using rates specified in the IRC. The IRC provides depreciation rate schedules, referred to as the modified accelerated cost recovery system (MACRS), which set annual depreciation rates for various asset classes. The depreciation rates allow greater depreciation in the early years of an asset's life relative to straight-line depreciation rates. Accelerated rates lead to greater tax deductible expenses and lower tax payments in the early years of the asset's life relative to straight-line depreciation, but lower tax deductions in later years.

For financial reporting purposes, however, firms can choose among a variety of depreciation methods, some accelerated and some not. Firms cannot use the MACRS rates for financial reporting purposes. Thus, the amount of depreciation expense recorded in the GAAP financial statements in any given year will be different from the depreciation deduction taken for tax purposes. And, the resulting value or basis of the asset, which is its cost less accumulated depreciation, will also be different. Over the life of the asset, however, the total cost of "consuming" the PP&E asset must be allocated to expense. This statement is true for both GAAP and tax purposes. Thus, the difference between tax and GAAP depreciation is a temporary difference.

---

[1] Note that the net book value of PP&E (the GAAP basis) and the tax basis will also be equal on the acquisition date.

The accounting for uncollectible accounts receivable is another example of an activity that generates a temporary difference. According to GAAP and consistent with the matching principle, firms use the allowance method to record bad debt expense as an estimate of uncollectible accounts in the period the sales revenue is recorded. For federal tax reporting purposes, however, firms generally use the specific charge-off method. Firms recognize a tax deduction only when they have exhausted all reasonable means of collection from a specific customer. Thus, the timing of the tax deduction is generally the same as the timing of the write-off under GAAP. In this case, in contrast to the previous depreciation example, the accumulated GAAP bad debts expense is higher than the accumulated tax deductions. As a result, the GAAP asset, net accounts receivable, will have a basis that is lower than the IRC basis. Over the life of a given account receivable portfolio, however, the amount estimated as bad debts will equal the amount written off.

Permanent differences

For some transactions or activities, the total amount of revenue or expense that the firm will include in taxable income over its life does not equal the total revenue or expense that will be recognized as GAAP pretax income in the financial statements. Such differences are called *permanent differences*. Permanent differences in revenue/expense recognition give rise to permanent differences in the GAAP/IRC basis of the assets/liabilities to which they relate.

A **PERMANENT DIFFERENCE** is a difference between pretax income and IRC taxable income that arises because one set of rules allows for the recognition of an expense or revenue while the other does not. Such items never reverse.

A common example of a permanent difference is travel and entertainment costs. While all of these costs must be shown on a firm's income statement as "expense" in the period incurred, only 80% of these expenses are deductible for tax purposes. Other examples include tax-exempt interest revenue, and income from foreign subsidiaries that is taxed at a different rate than U.S. income.

The following example illustrates a temporary difference and a permanent difference for Acme, Inc., which will be used to illustrate various calculations throughout the chapter.

Acme Inc. has two assets, a machine and a municipal bond. The machine was purchased on January 1, Year 1 for $100. The useful life of the machine is three years and there is no estimated salvage value. The firm uses straight-line depreciation for financial statement preparation, which results in annual GAAP depreciation expense of $33.30. Assume that Acme's machine belongs to the three year MACRS asset class with annual depreciation rates of 58.3%, 27.8%, and 13.9%.[2]

---

[2] MACRS rates depend on the asset being depreciated and the period in which the asset is placed in service. The rates assumed in this problem approximate those for three-year property placed in service in the first quarter of the year.

The municipal bond earns $10 interest per year, all of which is accrued (adding to the value of the bond as an asset). Interest on the bond is tax free.

Exhibit 1 shows the results of Acme's year 1 operations. The first column shows the computation of income according to GAAP and represents the amounts that would be reported on Acme's income statement. The second column shows the taxable revenues and tax deductible expenses measured according to the IRC.

Exhibit 1
Acme Inc., Summary information

	Year 1		Year 2		Year 3		3-Year Total	
	GAAP	IRC	GAAP	IRC	GAAP	IRC	GAAP	IRC
Sales	$200	$200	$250	$250	$280	$280		
Cost of goods sold	(120)	(120)	(140)	(140)	(160)	(160)		
Gross margin	80	80	110	110	120	120		
Deprecation expense	(33.30)	(58.30)	(33.30)	(27.80)	(33.40)	(13.90)	$(100.00)	$(100.00)
Interest income	10.00	-	10.00	-	10.00	-	30.00	-
Pretax income	56.70		86.70		96.60			
Taxable income		21.70		82.20		106.10		
Temporary difference (depreciation)	25.00		(5.50)		(19.50)		0.00	
Permanent difference (interest)	10.00		10.00		10.00		30.00	
Total difference between pretax and taxable income	35.00		4.50		(9.50)		30.00	
End-of-year basis of the machine	66.70	41.70	33.40	13.90	0.00	0.00		
Accumulated temporary difference in basis	25.00		19.50		0.00			
End-of-year basis of the bond	160.00	150.00	170.00	150.00	180.00	150.00		
Accumulated permanent difference in basis	10.00		20.00		30.00			

In this example, for simplicity, sales and cost of goods sold for Acme are the same for GAAP and IRC purposes.

GAAP depreciation expense for Acme differs from IRC depreciation expense. The different amounts reflect a difference between the straight-line depreciation rate of 33.3% per year and the annual depreciation rate mandated by the IRC. Although the GAAP and IRC depreciation expense is different each year, the total depreciation expense over all three years is the same. The temporary difference is positive in year 1 when GAAP depreciation is less than IRC depreciation and negative in years 2 and 3 when GAAP depreciation exceeds IRC depreciation. In this example, the GAAP asset basis (cost less accumulated depreciation) is greater than the tax basis in year 1, with the difference between the two decreasing over time. At the end of the asset's three year life, the difference in the basis is zero.

36

The bond interest is included in Acme's GAAP pretax income but it is not included in taxable income because it is not taxable according to the IRC. Each year there is a $10 permanent difference between GAAP pretax income and IRC taxable income. The GAAP basis of the bond includes the annual accrued interest receivable of $10. The IRC basis of the bond does not include the accrued interest because the interest income on the bond does not exist for tax purposes. Over the life of the asset (three years), the permanent difference in the basis is $30.

CALCULATING TAX EXPENSE, TAX ASSETS, AND TAX LIABILITIES

Tax expense

GAAP tax expense is reported on the income statement. It is also called the *"Provision for income taxes."* Consistent with the accrual method of accounting, GAAP tax expense represents the tax consequences of the current year's operations, regardless of whether the income related to those operations is reported for the current year under the IRC rules. That is, firms record an accrued expense (a tax liability) for taxes that will be paid in future periods when the income is reported to the IRS, but which are related to income that has already been recognized for GAAP purposes. Firms also record a prepaid amount (a tax asset) for taxes that are paid based on taxable income, but which are related to income that will be recognized in future periods under GAAP.

Thus, the provision for income taxes is the sum of two components:

1) Current taxes, which represent taxes related to the current year's <u>taxable income</u>, and

2) Deferred taxes, which are amounts that will be paid in future periods or which have been paid in past periods, but which represent the tax consequences of current period activities measured under GAAP.

Current taxes

Current taxes represent the firm's tax obligation related to its current year operations as reported to tax authorities based on the IRC revenue and expense recognition rules. Current taxes are a function of taxable income.

Current taxes = IRC taxable income × statutory tax rate

The "statutory" tax rate is the rate that is enacted by a governmental body (i.e., by statute). Firms pay federal income taxes based on federal statutory rates, and can pay taxes at different statutory rates in various states or in foreign countries.

For Acme Inc., assume a statutory tax rate of 40%. In year 1, Acme's current taxes are $8.70, calculated as IRC taxable income of $21.70 multiplied by the statutory tax rate of 40%. Year 2 and year 3 current taxes are calculated in a similar way, and are $32.90 and $42.40, respectively. GAAP pretax income does not affect current taxes.

Current taxes represent the total amount due to the Internal Revenue Service (or other tax authorities) *for the year*. Current taxes do not represent the amount that is due *at year end*. Firms generally make interim payments to various tax authorities throughout a year. Taxes payable at year end, which is included in liabilities on a firm's balance sheet, represent only the portion that is still due as of the end of the year. Exhibit 2 shows that Frontier includes taxes payable at year end in "other accrued expenses" on the balance sheet.

Exhibit 2
REAL WORLD EXCERPT: Presentation of Taxes Payable
FRONTIER AIRLINES

Excerpts from the Notes to the Financial Statements
(4) Other Accrued Expenses

The March 31, 2001 and 2000, other accrued expenses is comprised of the following:

	2001	2000
Accrued salaries and benefits	$11,769,806	$ 5,505,449
Income taxes payable	-	5,483,264
Federal excise taxes payable	2,720,977	3,664,429
Other	3,745,696	2,888,877
	$18,236,479	$17,542,019

Deferred taxes
Deferred taxes result from the temporary differences between IRC rules and GAAP rules. A deferred tax liability (DTL) represents the tax consequences of income recognized in the current year under GAAP that will not be recognized until a future year under IRC rules. A deferred tax asset (DTA) represents the tax consequences of income recognized for tax purposes in the current year that will not be recognized until a future year under GAAP. Permanent differences do not create deferred tax assets or liabilities because the firm will never have taxable income or tax deductible expenses associated with these amounts.

A *deferred tax liability* exists when the GAAP basis of an asset, such as PP&E, is *greater* than the IRC basis of that asset and the difference is temporary or when the GAAP basis of a liability, such as the reserve for warranty expense, is *less* than the IRC basis of that liability and the difference is temporary. For either of these situations to exist, it must be that the accumulated tax deductions that the firm has taken, such as for depreciation or warranty costs, are greater than the expense recognized for GAAP purposes. Thus, the firm has reported lower taxable income in past years relative to pretax income and paid lower taxes relative to the amount expensed. However, because the differences in the basis are temporary, they will have to reverse in a future period. When they do reverse, the firm will pay more taxes than it expenses. The obligation to pay these additional taxes is the deferred tax liability.

A *deferred tax asset* exists when the GAAP basis of an asset, such as accounts receivable, is *less* than the IRC basis of that asset and the difference is temporary or when the GAAP basis of a liability, such as compensation payable, is *greater* than the IRC basis of that liability and the difference is temporary. For either of these situations to exist, it must be that the accumulated tax deductions that the firm has taken, such as for bad debts expense or compensation costs, are less than the expense recognized for GAAP purposes. Thus, the firm has reported higher taxable income in past years relative to pretax income and paid higher taxes than the amount expensed. However, because the differences in the basis are temporary, they will have to reverse in a future period. When they do, the firm will pay less taxes than it expenses. The benefit of having "prepaid" these additional taxes is the deferred tax asset.

A **DEFERRED TAX LIABILITY** arises when the temporary difference between the GAAP basis of an asset (or liability) is greater than (or less than) the IRC basis.

A **DEFERRED TAX ASSET** arises when the temporary difference between the GAAP basis of an asset (or liability) is less than (or greater than) the IRC basis.

Item that creates temporary difference:	IRC basis >/< GAAP basis	Past IRC deductions >/< past GAAP expense	=
Asset (e.g., PP&E)	>	<	DTA
	<	>	DTL
Liability (e.g., warranty)	>	<	DTL
	<	>	DTA

Deferred tax assets also are generated by net operating loss carryforwards (NOLs), other loss carryforwards (e.g., capital loss carryforwards), or tax credits. Firms that have net losses in a given year can use these losses to offset future taxable income.[3] For each dollar of taxable loss that the firm can carry forward, it will create a DTA equal to the tax effect of that amount. The tax effect is the tax basis of the operating loss multiplied by the current period statutory tax rate. Tax credits generate DTAs equal to the amount of the credit.

The amount of the deferred tax liability or deferred tax asset related to the accumulated temporary difference between the GAAP basis and the IRC basis of a firm's assets or liabilities is the difference in the bases multiplied by the statutory tax rate.

Deferred tax asset or liability = difference in bases x statutory tax rate

Once the appropriate ending balance for each deferred tax asset and liability is determined, a firm computes the adjustment necessary to report the appropriate DTA or DTL on its balance sheet.

To illustrate the calculation of deferred tax asset and liabilities, consider Acme, Inc. again. The only temporary difference is the accounting for depreciation expense. Assume that the statutory tax rate is 40%.

Exhibit 3
Calculation of deferred tax liability

	Year 1		Year 2		Year 3		3-Year Total	
	GAAP	IRC	GAAP	IRC	GAAP	IRC	GAAP	IRC
Deprecation expense	$(33.30)	$(58.30)	$(33.30)	$(27.80)	$(33.40)	$(13.90)	$(100.00)	$(100.00)
End-of-year basis	66.70	41.70	33.40	13.90	0.00	0.00		
Difference in basis	25.00		19.50		0.00			
Statutory tax rate	40%		40%		40%			
End-of-year Deferred tax liability	$10.00		$7.80		$0.00			
Change for the year	**$10.00**		**$(2.20)**		**$(7.80)**			

In year 1, the end-of-the-year deferred tax liability ($10) equals the difference in basis ($25) multiplied by the statutory tax rate (40%). The beginning-of-the-year tax liability is zero, so deferred tax expense for year 1 is $10 and the

---

[3] Firms can carry losses forward 15 years to offset taxable income. Firms can carry losses back from two to five years depending on the year of the loss. Firms can also elect to carry forward all of the losses in a given year.

deferred tax liability account increases by $10. In year 2, the difference in basis decreases, which means that the deferred tax liability should also decrease. During year 2, taxes as reported to the IRS were greater than if they had been calculated based on GAAP income because tax deductible depreciation expense was less than GAAP depreciation expense. Thus, some of the taxes that were deferred in year 1 when IRC depreciation was greater than GAAP depreciation are effectively being paid in year 2. Note that at the end of year 3, the sum of temporary differences equals zero (the temporary difference created in year 1 have completely reversed) and both the difference in basis and the end-of-the-year deferred tax liability are equal to zero.

In any given year, a firm may create DTLs, reverse (pay) DTLs that were created in past years, create DTAs, and/or reverse (use up) DTAs created in past years. The net effect of all these changes to the deferred tax assets and liabilities is called *deferred taxes*. Deferred taxes are the second component of income tax expense; they can be either an expense or a benefit. Deferred taxes will be a net expense when taxes computed based on GAAP income are greater than taxes based on taxable income. Deferred taxes will be a net benefit when taxes computed based on GAAP income are less than taxes based on taxable income.

For financial reporting purposes, a deferred tax asset is carried at the amount of the undiscounted expected future benefit and a deferred tax liability is carried at the amount of the undiscounted expected future obligation. Unlike other long-term liabilities on a firm's balance sheet, DTLs are not carried at net present value.

To put all these terms and concepts together, consider the components of tax expense in journal entry format. Assume a firm has positive pretax income (under GAAP) and positive taxable income. The firm computes current taxes as the statutory tax rate multiplied by taxable income. The firm computes the adjustments necessary for each DTA and DTL. Income tax expense is the sum of current taxes (which increase the current taxes payable account), and deferred taxes (which is the sum of all adjustments to the DTA and DTL accounts).

> Income tax expense (plug)
> DTA (to create a deferred tax asset)
> DTL (to reverse an existing deferred tax liability)
> > DTA (to reverse an existing deferred tax asset)
> > DTL (to create a deferred tax liability)
> > Current taxes payable (taxable income * tax rate)

The debits and credits to create and reverse DTAs and DTLs in the journal entry above are computed to reflect the changes in the tax effects of temporary differences.

The journal entries for Acme would be as follows:

Year 1

Income tax expense (+E, -SE)	18.7	
Taxes payable (+L)		8.7
Deferred tax liabilities (+L)		10.0

Year 2

Income tax expense (+E, -SE)	30.7	
Deferred tax liabilities (-L)	2.2	
Taxes payable (+L)		32.9

Year 3

Income tax expense (+E, -SE)	34.6	
Deferred tax liabilities (-L)	7.8	
Taxes payable (+L)		42.4

Assets	=	Liabilities		+	Stockholders' Equity	
Year 1		Taxes payable	+8.7		Income tax expense	18.7
		Deferred tax liabilities	+10.0			
Year 2		Taxes payable	-2.2		Income tax expense	-30.7
		Deferred tax liabilities	+32.9			
Year 3		Taxes payable	-7.8		Income tax expense	-34.6
		Deferred tax liabilities	+42.4			

The credits to the taxes payable accounts are the current taxes for the year; the computation was discussed earlier in this section. The credit and subsequent debits to the deferred tax liability account represent the adjustment necessary to get the DTL account to the appropriate balance as shown in Exhibit 3.

Deferred tax assets and liabilities are always calculated using current tax rates. If new tax rates are enacted, the new rates are applied to the accumulated temporary differences to compute the appropriate DTA or DTL. As a result, the impact of the change in tax rates flows directly through income tax expense as an adjustment in the current period.

FINANCIAL ANALYSIS:
Effective tax rate

A firm's effective tax rate is tax expense as reported on the income statement divided by pretax income:

Effective tax rate = GAAP Tax expense/GAAP pretax income

Analysts commonly use the firm's effective tax rate to compute the tax effect of any income or expense-related item. The effective tax rate does <u>not</u> equal the statutory tax rate or the firm's marginal tax rate, which is the tax rate that would be paid on the firm's next dollar of income. It is impossible to compute a firm's marginal tax rate from publicly available data. The effective tax rate is often used as a proxy because the effective tax rate can be calculated using the income statement.

Using the income tax expense that Acme would report in its income statement (see the preceding journal entries) and Acme's pretax income, Acme's effective tax rate for years 1 – 3 would be:

Year 1: 18.7/56.7 = 33.0%
Year 2: 30.7/86.7 = 35.4%
Year 3: 34.6/96.6 = 35.8%

The reason for the difference between the statutory rate and the effective rate is permanent differences.

The taxes of $18.7 for year 1 differ from the amount you would expect based on multiplying pretax income by the statutory tax rate of 40% (56.7*40% = $22.7). The difference of $4 is the tax consequence of the $10 permanent difference related to the municipal bond.

You can also think about the effect of this permanent difference on the effective tax rate in percentage terms. Acme's effective tax rate is 33.0% in year 1. The effective rate differs from the statutory rate of 40% by 7.0%. The 7% difference equals the $4 tax consequences of the municipal bond income divided by pretax GAAP income of $56.7.

The fact that permanent differences generate a difference between the statutory rate and the effective rate is important because a required footnote disclosure is a reconciliation of the two rates. That footnote reconciliation will indicate a firm's permanent differences. The footnote may be presented in dollar terms (e.g., a $4 tax effect) or in percentage terms (e.g., a 7% effect).

Valuation allowances against DTAs

Firms are required to record a valuation allowance for the portion of deferred tax assets that if it is "more likely than not" that some portion of the DTA will not be realized in a future period. A valuation allowance against deferred tax assets is analogous to the allowance for uncollectible accounts on accounts receivable. It represents the amount that the firm may not realize in terms of lower tax payments in future periods.

A firm's ability to realize the benefits of a deferred tax asset depends on it having taxable income in future periods. Thus, the determination of the need for and amount of a valuation allowance requires a firm to predict the availability of future taxable income, which is clearly subjective. Firms frequently record a 100% valuation allowance against DTAs associated with loss carryforwards and tax credits, although this is not required. The change in the valuation allowance is included in income from continuing operations as part of income tax expense.

TAX REPORTING IN THE FINANCIAL STATEMENTS AND THE FOOTNOTES

The financial statements for Frontier Airlines illustrate tax reporting. In a firm's income statement, income tax expense is reported as a separate line item after the subtotal for pretax income. It represents the total of current and deferred tax expense. Frontier Airlines reports income tax expense for the fiscal year ended March 31, 2001, of $33.465 million after income before income tax expense (pretax income) of $88.332 million.

In a firm's balance sheet, there are five accounts that may appear related to taxes. First, firms can separately report income taxes payable, which represents the liability for taxes still owed as of year end, after accounting for the interim cash payments made to tax authorities. Frontier Airlines indicates that taxes payable is included in other accrued liabilities on the balance sheet (see footnote 4—Exhibit 2). The amounts payable at March 31, 2001, and March 31, 2000, were $0 and $5.483 million respectively.

The other four accounts you might see on a balance sheet relate to deferred taxes: 1) current deferred tax assets, 2) current deferred tax liabilities, 3) noncurrent deferred tax assets, and 4) noncurrent deferred tax liabilities. DTAs or DTLs are classified as "current" ("noncurrent") when they are related to current (noncurrent) assets or liabilities on the balance sheet or, if they do not relate to a specific asset or liability on the balance sheet, when they are (are not) expected to reverse in the coming year. The level of aggregation of these four separate accounts on the balance sheet varies across firms. The current amounts may be included in "other" current assets and "other" current liabilities when they are immaterial. In most cases, you will need to read the tax footnote to figure out the total deferred tax assets and liabilities and the current and noncurrent portions.

Frontier separately reports current DTAs of $1,506,218 and noncurrent DTLs of $1,999,553 on its balance sheet. These amounts agree with the totals reported in Panel 3 of Frontier's tax footnote (shown in Exhibit 7), which indicates that the current DTAs of $1.5 million are the firm's only DTAs and the noncurrent DTLs of $2 million are the only DTLs.

The supplemental disclosures to the statement of cash flows report taxes paid during the year (see Exhibit 4). These amounts could represent payments of the prior year's liability or interim payments related to the current year tax provision.

Exhibit 4
REAL WORLD EXCERPT:
FRONTIER AIRLINES Statements of Cash Flows -- EXCERPTS
Years ended March 31, 2001, 2000, and 1999

	2001	2000	1999
Cash flows from operating activities:			
Net income	$ 54,867,773	$ 27,009,253	$ 30,566,060
Adjustments to reconcile net income to net cash provided by operating activities:			
Employee stock ownership plan compensation expense	1,411,876	895,412	848,875
Depreciation and amortization	5,618,200	3,725,697	2,705,255
Loss on sale of equipment	56,800	-	3,867
Deferred tax expense (benefit)	**1,146,015**	**5,459,468**	**(6,010,648)**
Changes in operating assets and liabilities:			
Restricted investments	(5,639,400)	402,000	(425,301)
Trade receivables	(6,060,773)	(5,260,797)	(5,268,715)
Security, maintenance and other deposits	(16,207,351)	(8,288,288)	(6,968,057)
Prepaid expenses	(3,462,229)	(1,947,017)	(1,596,140)
Inventories	(1,837,152)	(1,031,267)	(39,606)
Accounts payable	7,215,154	396,675	346,488
Air traffic liability	18,144,400	15,631,145	9,977,251
Other accrued expenses	694,460	10,084,065	5,758,840
Accrued maintenance expense	16,578,273	8,130,957	6,057,944
Net cash provided by operating activities	72,526,046	55,207,303	35,956,113

Supplemental Disclosure of Cash Flow Information
Cash Paid During the Year for:

	2001	2000	1999
Interest	$ 94,393	$ 119,496	$ 302,503
Taxes	**$ 21,926,000**	**$ 3,005,000**	**$ -**

Paragraphs 43 – 49 of SFAS 109 provide detailed guidance on required disclosures related to income taxes. Most firms implement the disclosure requirements in a fairly standard format that includes three tables in a tax footnote.

1. One table shows the current and deferred portions of total GAAP tax expense for all years for which an income statement is presented. It indicates the debits and credits to income tax expense, taxes payable, and the deferred tax accounts for the year. It may also disaggregate foreign, state and local taxes.

2. A second table reconciles the effective tax rate to the U.S. federal statutory tax rate (e.g., 40% compared to 33.0% for Acme in year 1) or reconciles taxes based on the effective tax rate (in dollars) to taxes based on the U.S. federal statutory tax rate. The reconciliation is shown for all years for which an income statement is presented.

3. A third table reports the balances of DTLs and DTAs at each balance sheet date. Recall that these balances represent the tax effects of the accumulated temporary differences as of the balance sheet date. The changes in these accounts represent the tax effects of the current year's temporary differences.

Note that firms do not necessarily present the tables in the same order, but almost all tax footnotes include (at least) these three tables to meet the disclosure requirements.

Exhibits 5, 6, and 7 show each of these tables for Frontier Airlines, respectively. We will explain the information that is reflected in each of Frontier's tables and how it can be used by analysts.

Exhibit 5
REAL WORLD EXCERPT
FRONTIER AIRLINES - Income Tax footnote - Panel 1

Income tax expense (benefit) for the years ended March 31, 2001, 2000, and 1999 consists of:

	Current	Deferred	Total
Year ended March 31, 2001:			
U.S. Federal	$28,441,039	$ 1,008,515	$29,449,554
State and local	3,877,611	137,500	4,015,111
	$32,318,650	$ 1,146,015	$ 33,464,665
Year ended March 31, 2000:			
U.S. Federal	$ 9,785,064	$ 4,726,153	$14,511,217
State and local	1,811,343	631,814	2,443,157
	$11,596,407	$ 5,357,967	$16,954,374
Year ended March 31, 1999:			
U.S. Federal	$ 531,077	$ (5,244,134)	$ (4,713,057)
State and local	-	(766,513)	(766,513)
	$ 531,077	$ (6,010,647)	$ (5,479,570)

For the year ended March 31, 2001, the first panel of Frontier Airlines' income tax footnote (Exhibit 5) shows total tax expense of $33,464,665, which is the amount reported on the income statement. It indicates that $32,318,650 of this amount is related to the current year's operations as reported to tax authorities, and the remainder ($1,146,015) is deferred tax expense. These numbers can also be shown in journal entry format:

Income tax expense (+E, –SE)	33,464,665
Deferred tax assets/liabilities (-A/+L)	1,146,015
Taxes payable (+L)	32,318,650

Recall that the $32.319 million represents Frontier's total taxes to be paid related to 2001. However, it is not the amount <u>payable</u> at March 31, 2001. Frontier made interim tax payments throughout fiscal 2001. Footnote 4 of Frontier's financial statements (see Exhibit 2) reports that taxes payable is $5.483 million at the beginning of the fiscal year and $0 at March 31, 2001. Thus, Frontier paid $37.802 million of taxes during 2001 {$5.483 + $32.319 – $0}. The amount paid includes estimated quarterly payments related to the 2001 tax obligation of $32.319.

The $1.146 million in the previous journal entry is the net change in current and noncurrent deferred tax assets and liabilities. (We will show the details about which deferred tax assets and liabilities increased or decreased later.) The $1.146 million is also shown on the statement of cash flows in the operating section as a reconciling item (see Exhibit 4). This adjustment on the statement of cash flows, together with the adjustment for the change in income taxes payable (included in other accrued expenses), reconciles the tax expense component of net income to taxes paid, which are an operating cash outflow. Firms, like Frontier, may also separately report domestic versus foreign taxes or even federal versus state and local taxes.

Exhibit 6
REAL WORLD EXCERPT
FRONTIER AIRLINES - Income Tax footnote
Panel 2

The differences between the Company's effective rate for income taxes and the federal statutory rate are shown in the following table:

	2001	2000	1999
Income tax expense at the statutory rate	(35%)	(35%)	(35%)
Decrease in valuation allowance	-	-	60%
State and local income tax, net of federal income tax benefit	(3%)	(3%)	(3%)
Nondeductible expenses	-	(1%)	-
	(38%)	(39%)	22%

The second panel within Frontier's tax footnote (Exhibit 6) reconciles the effective tax rate to the U.S. federal statutory tax rate or taxes based on the effective tax rate to taxes based on the U.S. federal statutory tax rate. The effective tax rate will differ from the U.S federal tax rate because not all taxes are based on the U.S. federal rate, and tax rates in other jurisdictions may vary. Also, the effective tax rate will differ from the statutory rate if the firm utilizes net operating loss carryforwards. Finally, the effective rate will differ from the U.S. federal tax rate because of permanent differences. Hence, this reconciliation indicates the major permanent differences between GAAP and IRC pretax income for the firm.

Note that the table describes the *tax effect* of the noted reconciling items, such as a permanent difference. It does not show the amount of the permanent difference.

The second table within the Frontier income tax footnote shows Frontier's reconciliation of the U.S. federal statutory rate (35%) to Frontier's effective tax rate of 38%. The first important item to note is that Frontier's effective tax rate for 2001 is, in fact, 38%.

Effective tax rate	=	GAAP tax expense	/	pretax income
37.9%	=	$33.465 million	/	$88.332 million

In fiscal 2001, there is only one reconciling item between the U.S federal rate and the effective rate: 3% related to state and local taxes. Frontier incurs income tax expense for state and local taxes in addition to its expense for federal income taxes. These are included in GAAP tax expense, and thus in the calculation of the effective tax rate, but the 35% statutory rate is for federal taxes only. Frontier has no permanent differences in 2001. In 2000, Frontier had permanent differences due to "Nondeductible expenses," which are amounts that are expensed under GAAP and which reduce pretax income but which cannot be deducted as an expense under the IRC rules. One example noted previously is the 20% of travel and entertainment expenses that is not deductible. Permanent differences for nondeductible expenses increase the effective rate relative to the statutory rate by 1.0%. The tax effect of the permanent differences is:

Tax rate effect	×	pretax book income	=	Tax $ effect
1%	×	$88.332 million	=	$883,320

This amount represents the taxes Frontier paid as a result of not being able to deduct the "nondeductible expenses".

The amount of the nondeductible expenses is computed as follows:

Tax $ effect	/	Tax rate	=	Nondeductible expenses
$883,320	/	35%	=	$2.523 million

Exhibit 7
REAL WORLD EXCERPT
FRONTIER AIRLINES - Income Tax footnote
Panel 3

The tax effects of temporary differences that give rise to significant portions of the deferred tax assets (liabilities) at March 31, 2001 and 2000, are presented below:

	2001	2000
Deferred tax assets:		
Accrued vacation and insurance liabilities not deductible for tax purposes	$ 1,355,226	$ 1,041,000
Inventory reserves	856	134,000
Other	150,136	136,000
Total gross deferred tax assets	1,506,218	1,311,000
Deferred tax liabilities:		
Equipment depreciation and amortization	(1,999,553)	(556,000)
Book/tax difference on warranty treatment	-	(102,000)
Total gross deferred tax liabilities	(1,999,553)	(658,000)
Net deferred tax asset (liability)	$ (493,335)	$ 653,000

The net deferred tax asset (liability) are reflected in accompanying balance sheet as follows:

	2001	2000
Current deferred tax assets	$1,506,218	$1,136,194
Non-current deferred tax liability	(1,999,553)	(483,514)
Net deferred tax asset (liability)	$ (493,335)	$ 652,680

The Company recognized an income tax benefit of $5,479,570 in 1999 attributable to the probable realization of its remaining income tax loss carryforwards for which a valuation allowance had previously been recorded. The Company's net operating loss carryforwards of approximately $11,891,000 and alternative minimum tax credits of approximately $525,000 at March 31, 1999, were fully utilized to reduce federal regular income taxes during the year ended March 31, 2000.

The third panel within the tax footnote (Exhibit 7) presents the balances of the current and noncurrent deferred tax assets and liabilities at each date for which a balance sheet is presented. The table shows DTLs and DTAs for each major asset or liability, such as PP&E or insurance obligations, that has a different GAAP basis and IRC basis due to a temporary difference.

The balances of the DTA and DTL accounts represent the tax effect of the accumulated temporary differences between the GAAP basis and the IRC basis of each asset or liability. The change in the deferred tax asset or liability accounts from the beginning of the year to the end of the year reflects the tax effect of the temporary difference for that year.

The third panel in Frontier's tax footnote shows total deferred tax assets of $1,506,218 and total deferred tax liabilities of $1,999,553 at March 31, 2001. We noted these amounts previously on the balance sheet in current assets and noncurrent liabilities. The table indicates that there are three sources of DTAs: Accrued vacation and insurance liabilities that are not deductible for tax purposes, inventory reserves, and "other." There are two sources of DTLs: Depreciation and amortization, and the accounting for warrants. Since these five items create deferred tax assets and liabilities, all of them are temporary differences between GAAP and IRC revenue/expense recognition.

The changes in the deferred tax accounts for fiscal 2001 are:

		2001		2000		Change
Increase in deferred tax assets	=	1,506,218	–	$1,311,000	=	$195,218
Increase in deferred tax liabilities	=	$1,999,553	–	$658,000	=	$1,341,553

The net change is $1.146 million ($1.341 million – $0.195 million). We have seen the $1.146 million before. It is the deferred portion of the income tax expense in the first table of Frontier's footnote (see Exhibit 5).

For many firms, this calculation won't work out so nicely. The change in the deferred tax assets and deferred tax liabilities accounts will not equal the deferred tax expense for the period. One major reason is that DTAs and DTLs may be generated as part of an acquisition of another firm. Likewise, when a firm divests of operations, DTAs and DTLs associated with the operation will be reversed. The changes in DTAs and DTLs related to acquisitions and divestitures are not included in the deferred portion of income tax expense.

One source of Frontier's DTLs is equipment depreciation and amortization. There is a temporary difference between the GAAP basis and the IRC basis of equipment (and other amortized assets) due to differences in the recognition of depreciation and amortization for GAAP and IRC purposes. The temporary difference creates a DTL of $556,000 at March 31, 2000, and of $1,999,553 at March 31, 2001.

We can compute the difference between the GAAP basis and the IRC basis of the depreciable assets at each balance sheet date.

The $1,999,553 is the tax effect of the accumulated temporary difference between the GAAP basis of Frontier's depreciable assets and their IRC basis. Thus, the accumulated temporary difference in basis on March 31, 2001, is $1,999,553/0.35 = $5,713,009. The temporary difference has generated a deferred tax liability at March 31, 2001, which implies that Frontier has already recorded tax expense for amounts to be paid in future periods. Thus, the accumulated IRC deductions to date have been greater than the GAAP expenses for depreciation and the IRC basis of the depreciable assets is less than the tax basis.

We can also compute the amount of the temporary difference between GAAP depreciation and IRC depreciation for the fiscal year 2001. Note the distinction between this computation and the previous one. We are now computing the temporary difference during the year rather than the temporary difference between the GAAP and IRC basis, which is the accumulation of temporary differences to date.

The difference between GAAP depreciation and the depreciation deducted for tax purposes during fiscal 2001 is computed from the change in the DTL. During 2001, the DTL related to depreciation increased by $1.444 million from $556,000 to $1,999,553. This amount represents the <u>tax effect</u> of the current year's temporary difference between GAAP and IRC depreciation. Therefore, the temporary difference between GAAP and IRC depreciation is $4,124.6 = $1,443.6/0.35.[4]

Was GAAP depreciation higher or lower than IRC depreciation for 2001? To answer this question, we will have to analyze the direction of the change in the deferred tax account. In this case, the temporary difference for the year increased a DTL. An increase in a DTL implies that Frontier will be paying more taxes in future periods than it expenses in those periods. If Frontier will be paying more in future periods, then it must be paying less than it expenses in the current period since the difference is temporary. So, IRC taxes related to depreciation are less than GAAP tax expense related to depreciation. Taxes will be lower when income is lower, so it must be the case that IRC taxable income is less than GAAP pretax income (associated with depreciation). Since depreciation is an expense, IRC pretax income is less than GAAP pretax income related to this item only if IRC depreciation expense is greater than GAAP depreciation expense. In other words, depreciation deductions on

---

[4] This calculation is appropriate for Frontier because Frontier did not acquire or divest of any DTAs or DTLs. If they had, the change in the DTAs and DTLs for the year would include the effects of the acquisition and the divestiture, in addition to the tax effects of the temporary difference.

Frontier's tax return for 2001 must be greater than depreciation expense included in Frontier's income statement by $4,124.6.

Frontier Airlines does not have a valuation allowance. If Frontier had a valuation allowance, it would be shown as a reduction of the DTAs. The absence of a valuation allowance indicates that, in the opinion of Frontier management, it is more likely than not that Frontier will be able to realize its deferred tax assets. Frontier reports in Exhibit 7 that it reduced a valuation allowance that had "previously been recorded" to zero in 1999. It must be the case that in 1999 it became more likely than not that the DTAs could be realized. As Frontier notes in Exhibit 7, the reversal of the valuation allowance reduced reported income tax expense in 1999 (see the effect of the reversal in Exhibit 5).

CHAPTER TAKE-AWAYS

1. **Tax expense on the income statement is not equal to a firm's tax obligation for the year.** Tax expense is computed as a function of income measured under GAAP; the current tax obligation is computed as a function of taxable income, and the Internal Revenue Code sets the rules for the computation of taxable income.

2. **Deferred tax assets and liabilities are the accounts used to accrue differences between taxes expensed and taxes paid.** Temporary differences create deferred tax assets and liabilities.

3. **The effective tax rate is tax expense divided by GAAP pretax income.** Permanent differences cause the effective tax rate to differ from the statutory tax rate.

4. **Firms present (in reasonably consistent formats) three important pieces of information in their tax footnotes.** Three tables within the footnote show a summary of the current and deferred portion of income tax expense, a reconciliation of the effective tax rate to the statutory tax rate (which provides information about permanent differences), and the balances of deferred tax assets and deferred tax liabilities at each balance sheet date (which provide information about temporary differences).

EXERCISES

E2-1 Understanding Changes in Deferred Tax Assets

At the beginning of the fiscal year, the GAAP basis of an asset is greater than the IRC basis of that asset by $100 due to differences in depreciation rates. At the end of the fiscal year, the GAAP basis of the asset is greater than the IRC basis by $60.

Required:

Calculate the difference between GAAP depreciation expense and IRC depreciation. Is GAAP depreciation expense higher or lower than IRC depreciation?

E2-2 Calculating Tax Expense and Deferred Tax Assets and Liabilities

ABC Corp. has one asset and one liability that have temporary differences between the GAAP basis and the IRC basis. Assume no valuation allowances are necessary against DTAs and that the statutory tax rate is 40%. Use the information in the table below to answer the required questions.

Required:

1. What is the net deferred tax asset or deferred tax liability that ABC Corp. will show on its balance sheet for years 1–3?

2. How much GAAP income tax expense will ABC Corp. report for years 1-3? Separately calculate current and deferred taxes.

	Year 0		Year 1		Year 2		Year 3	
	GAAP	IRC	GAAP	IRC	GAAP	IRC	GAAP	IRC
Asset Basis (End-of-year)	800	700	600	400	450	180	200	0
Liability Basis (End-of-year)	60	65	68	72	80	85	90	88
IRC pre-tax income				420		160		550

E2-3 Creating a Tax Footnote: Acme Inc.

Use the information contained in the series of Acme Inc. examples throughout the chapter to prepare a tax footnote for Acme for years 1 and 2 that includes all required disclosures.

E2-4 Changes in Sources of DTAs/DTLs: Acme Inc. year 2 machine sale

Assume that Acme's operations remain as presented in the chapter for year 1. However, on January 1, year 2, Acme sells its machine for $50. All other activities during year 2 are the same as presented. For both GAAP and IRC purposes, the gain or loss is equal to the sales proceeds less the basis of the PP&E.

1. What is the year-2 journal entry to record the sale of the equipment on the GAAP books?
2. What is the GAAP gain or loss related to the sale? What is the tax gain or loss?
3. What is total income tax expense for year 2? What is the current portion? Deferred?

PROBLEMS

P2-1 Comprehensive Income Tax Problem

ABC Wholesaler Co. has a strategy of selling to high credit risk customers (at premium prices). ABC's customers tend to pay late, typically 3-5 months after receiving the goods. A large percentage of ABC's customers default. ABC estimates bad debt reserves in accordance with GAAP. ABC uses the specific charge off method for IRC purposes.

ABC also has an intangible asset, goodwill, that it amortizes on a straight line basis for GAAP purposes. This goodwill is not (i.e., never) deductible for IRC purposes.

The summary financial statements of ABC for years 3–5 for both GAAP and IRC purposes, are presented below. The basis of accounts receivable and goodwill are also included. Assume that the statutory tax rate is 35%.

	Year 3		Year 4		Year 5	
	GAAP	IRC	GAAP	IRC	GAAP	IRC
Sales	840	840	780	780	960	960
Cost of goods sold	(420)	(420)	(400)	(400)	(460)	(460)
Gross margin	420	420	380	380	500	500
Bad debt expense	(13)	(20)	(18)	(12)	(30)	(42)
Goodwill amortization	(25)	-	(25)	-	(25)	-
Pre-tax income	382	400	337	368	445	458
Accounts receivable basis (End-of-year)	270	290	255	281	308	322
Goodwill basis (End-of-year)	450	0	425	0	400	0

1. Compute the balances of DTAs and DTLs, if any, for years 3-5.
2. Compute current taxes, deferred taxes and total GAAP tax expense for years 4 and 5.
3. Compute the effective tax rate for years 4 and 5.
4. Prepare ABC Wholesaler's tax footnote for the year 5 financial statements.

P2-2 Valley National Bancorp

Refer to the excerpt from note 14 to Valley National Bancorp's 2001 financial statements shown below. Draw on your knowledge of the GAAP treatment of "Investment Securities Available for Sale" to explain why Investment Securities Available for Sale produces a deferred tax asset in year 2000 and a deferred tax liability in year 2001.

Valley National Bancorp – Excerpt from Note 14

The tax effects of temporary differences that gave rise to deferred tax assets and liabilities as of December 31, 2001 and 2000, are as follows:

	2001	2000
	(in thousands)	
Deferred tax assets:		
Allowance for loan losses	$25,619	$21,715
Investment securities available for sale	—	1,494
State privilege year taxes	304	—
Non-accrual loan interest	282	182
Other	7,213	7,623
Total deferred tax assets	33,418	31,014
Deferred tax liabilities:		
Tax over book depreciation	286	2,476
Investment securities available for sale	11,300	—
Purchase accounting adjustments	133	212
Unearned discount on investments	255	188
State privilege year taxes	—	34
Other	3,723	5,121
Total deferred tax liabilities	15,697	8,031
Net deferred tax asset	$17,721	$22,983

Based upon taxes paid and projections of future taxable income, management believes that it is more likely than not that the net deferred tax asset will be realized.

CASES AND PROJECTS

C2-1 Understanding Income Tax Disclosures

Refer to the International Game Technology (IGT) income tax footnote below and answer the following questions. Fiscal 2001 refers to the year ending September 29, 2001.

1. What is the effective tax rate for fiscal 2001? What is the statutory tax rate for fiscal 2001?
2. What is the amount of income tax expense IGT reported on its income statement for fiscal 2001? What is the amount IGT reported as income taxes on tax returns for fiscal 2001?
3. Which item created the largest <u>reduction</u> in IGT's effective tax rate relative to the statutory rate in fiscal 2001? Explain in your own words what you think this item is.
4. As of September 29, 2001, total PP&E at cost was $365,135 and accumulated depreciation according to GAAP was $158,788. What was IGT's accumulated depreciation related to PP&E for IRC purposes as of September 29, 2001?
5. Assume that "Reserves not currently deductible" applies only to the Allowance for Doubtful Accounts. What is the difference between the tax basis of net accounts receivable at September 30, 2001, and its book basis? Was the GAAP basis or the IRCV basis higher? Explain.
6. Is the difference in GAAP and IRC accounting for "Goodwill and other intangibles" permanent or temporary? Explain.
7. Is it more likely than not that IGT will realize the benefits of its deferred tax assets?
8. Is the change in net deferred tax assets and liabilities accounted for by the deferred tax expense for fiscal 2001? If not, what is a possible explanation for the difference?

EXCERPTS FROM FOOTNOTES TO THE FINANCIAL STATEMENTS

International Games Technology

15. Income Taxes

SFAS No. 109 requires recognition of deferred tax assets and liabilities for the expected future tax consequences of events that have been included in the financial statements or tax returns. Deferred income taxes reflect the net tax effects of (a) temporary differences between the carrying amounts of assets and liabilities for financial reporting purposes and the amounts used for income tax purposes, and (b) operating loss and tax credit carry forwards. We determine the net current and noncurrent deferred tax assets or liabilities separately for federal, state, and foreign jurisdictions.

The effective income tax rates differ from the statutory U.S. federal income tax rates as follows for the years ended:

(Dollars in thousands)	September 29, 2001 Amount	Rate	September 30, 2000 Amount	Rate	October 2, 1999 Amount	Rate
Taxes at federal statutory rate	$118,815	35.0%	$85,745	35.0%	$35,488	35.0%
Foreign subsidiaries tax	3,615	1.1	2,410	0.9	3,657	3.6
State income tax, net	5,307	1.5	5,109	2.3	2,670	2.6
Research and development credits	(3,167)	(0.9)	(750)	(0.3)	(2,192)	(2.2)
Valuation allowance, foreign subsidiaries	2,769	0.8	2,063	0.7	6,067	6.0
Expiration of tax contingencies	-	-	(850)	(0.3)	(5,344)	(5.3)
Adjustment to estimated income tax accruals	-	-	(3,010)	(1.2)	(3,306)	(3.3)
Other, net	(1,802)	(0.5)	(2,522)	(1.1)	(959)	(0.8)
Provision for income taxes	$125,537	37.0%	$88,195	36.0%	$36,081	35.6%

Components of our provision for income taxes were as follows for the years ended:

	September 29, 2001	September 30, 2000	October 2, 1999
(Dollars in thousands)			
Current			
Federal	$127,611	$80,893	$(11,602)
State	8,652	5,645	358
Foreign	4,698	4,478	9,118
Total current	140,961	91,016	(2,126)
Deferred			
Federal	(14,162)	(2,270)	30,761
State	(1,631)	222	1,566
Foreign	369	(773)	5,880
Total deferred	(15,424)	(2,821)	38,207
Provision for income taxes	$125,537	$88,195	$ 36,081

Significant components of our deferred tax assets and liabilities are detailed in the table below. Our valuation allowance relates to uncertainty of realization on deferred tax assets in IGT-Australia and IGT-Japan.

(Dollars in thousands)	September 29, 2001	September 30, 2000
Current deferred tax assets		
Reserves not currently deductible	$ 20,267	$ 22,228
Unrealized loss on currency translation adjustments	5,408	4,582
Foreign subsidiaries	138	652
Unrealized loss on investment securities	552	327
Other	3,688	1,297
Net current deferred tax assets	30,053	29,086
Non-current deferred tax assets		
Reserves not currently deductible	-	566
Reserves for proprietary gaming	95,639	69,869
Foreign subsidiaries	11,182	8,268
State income taxes	6,563	4,932
Goodwill and other intangibles	25,766	28,020
Net operating loss carry forwards	9,801	-
Other	2,276	1,246
Non-current deferred tax liabilities		
Difference between book and tax basis of property	(4,950)	(4,036)
Other	(1,650)	(3,065)
Total net non-current deferred tax assets	144,627	105,800
Valuation allowance	(10,899)	(8,130)
Net non-current deferred tax assets	133,728	97,670
Net deferred tax assets	$163,781	$126,756

C2-2 Understanding Income Tax Disclosures

Refer to the Ann Taylor Stores Corporation income tax footnote below and answer the following questions. Note that the statutory tax rate is 35%. Fiscal 2002 refers to the year ending February 2, 2002, and fiscal 2001 refers to the year ending February 3, 2001.

1. Is Ann Taylor's effective rate higher or lower than the statutory rate? Explain.
2. What is the amount of income tax expense Ann Taylor reported on its income statement for fiscal 2001? What is the amount Ann Taylor reported as income taxes on tax returns for fiscal 2001?
3. Is the difference between the GAAP and IRC basis of intangibles that is associated with non-deductible amortization of goodwill permanent or temporary? Explain.
4. Is the change in net deferred tax assets and liabilities accounted for by the deferred tax expense for fiscal 2001? If not, what are some possible explanations for the difference?
5. Draw on your knowledge of the GAAP treatment of expense accruals to explain why "Accrued Expenses" result in a deferred tax asset for Ann Taylor.
6. Assume Ann Taylor's depreciation expense according to GAAP was $43,529 for fiscal 2002. What was the amount of IRC depreciation expense for fiscal 2002?
7. What is the difference between the GAAP and IRC basis of inventory? Is the GAAP basis higher or lower than the IRC basis? Explain.

Ann Taylor Stores Corporation

10. Income Taxes

The provision for income taxes for the fiscal years ended February 2, 2002, February 3, 2001, and January 29, 2000, consists of the following:

	FISCAL YEARS ENDED		
(in thousands)	FEB. 2, 2002	FEB. 3, 2001	JAN. 29, 2000
Federal:			
Current	$27,492	$38,082	$41,682
Deferred	(4,359)	(3,047)	(3,033)
Total federal	23,133	35,035	38,649
State and local:			
Current	2,589	6,476	11,856
Deferred	(756)	(817)	(809)
Total state and local...	1,833	5,659	11,047
Foreign:			
Current	591	471	525
Deferred	---	(130)	---
Total foreign	591	341	525
Total	$25,557	$41,035	$50,221

The reconciliation between the provision for income taxes and the provision for income taxes at the federal statutory rate for the fiscal years ended February 2, 2002, February 3, 2001, and January 29, 2000, is as follows:

	Fiscal Years Ended		
(in thousands, except percentages)	February 2, 2002	February 3, 2001	January 29, 2000
Income before income taxes and extraordinary loss	$ 54,662	$ 93,398	$ 115,714
Federal statutory rate	35%	35%	35%
Provision for income taxes at federal statutory rate	$ 19,132	$ 32,689	$ 40,500
State and local income taxes, net of federal income tax benefit	2,916	4,751	6,278
Non-deductible amortization of goodwill	3,500	3,500	3,500
Earnings of foreign subsidiaries	29	78	79
Other	(20)	17	(136)
Provision for income taxes	$ 25,557	$ 41,035	$ 50,221

The tax effects of significant items comprising the Company's deferred tax assets as of February 2, 2002, and February 3, 2001, are as follows:

(in thousands)	FEB. 2, 2002	FEB. 3, 2001
Current:		
Inventory	$ 5,929	$ 4,375
Accrued expenses	6,666	3,364
Real estate	(2,819)	(2,087)
Total current	$ 9,776	$ 5,652
Noncurrent:		
Accrued expenses	$ ---	$ 983
Depreciation and amortization	(1,970)	(2,616)
Rent expense	6,057	5,510
Other	765	(16)
Total noncurrent	$ 4,852	$ 3,861

Income taxes provided reflect the current and deferred tax consequences of events that have been recognized in the Company's consolidated financial statements or tax returns. U.S. federal income taxes are provided on unremitted foreign earnings, except those that are considered permanently reinvested, which at February 2, 2002, amounted to approximately $6,803,000. However, if these earnings were not considered permanently reinvested, under current law, the incremental tax on such undistributed earnings would be approximately $2,148,000.